To See the Wind

To See the Wind

MARIE WALSTON

Judson Press, Valley Forge

TO SEE THE WIND

Library of Congress Cataloging in Publication Data

Walston, Marie.

To see the wind.

1. Children, Blind. I. Title.
HV1792.C58W3 362.7′8′41 74-3231
ISBN 0-8170-0622-2

While this book is a story of the author's personal experience, all names of persons included in the account have been changed.

Printed in U.S.A.

TABLE OF CONTENTS

PROLOGUE

State Highway 7 follows a zigzag course north and south through the middle of Arkansas. It begins in the Ozark mountain highlands, rides the ridges to Jasper, and then climbs steeply into some of the roughest country in the state. Newton County, with its village seat, has never had a train track and, until recent years, no all-weather roads.

Though most of the Ozark mountains are gently rounded, these in Newton County fall away in breathtaking descents and present wide views of tumbled forest that fade into a distant haze. This is the area which I called home during the happy years of my childhood, even though these same times encompassed the hard years of the Depression Era which gripped this country during the 1930s.

I remember my childhood names for medicinal plants and the little wild flowers. I remember the fragance of muscadines, pawpaws, and wild plums in bloom. I remember the dogwood, the redbud, and the wood violets that created a special mood in springtime; while the blaze of sumac and gum, mingled with cedar and the yellow of hickory, made a kaleidoscopic fall.

I remember the rail fences with corners locked with upright stakes, and I remember the horse troughs made from hollow logs that sat beside dug wells. Though it was the beginning of the New Deal Era, many things bespoke the isolation that the mountains forced upon the inhabitants of that region.

Elderly people reproduced the pioneer "bar" for bear, and "thar" for there. Women wore sunbonnets, and the men walked with a loose-kneed gait that was remarkably fast, whether they were striking out for town, fourteen miles away, or just making a circle to kill a few squirrels.

Since Newton County was very steep, most of the farmers cultivated the hill tops. In that onionskin soil, no deeper than the grass roots, they grew sorghum cane, vegetables, and spindly corn. They had a few hogs and a few cows. Come winter, hams and shoulders dangled from the smokehouse ceiling. Cellars contained dried apples, potatoes, molasses, and onions. Strings of red peppers and dried green beans lined the walls of the dogtrot halls. The farmers were nearly independent of the outside world.

Near our farm a spring-fed creek trinkled into the Buffalo River. For more than a million years, the Buffalo had been a wild, free river. During its millennia of roaring and murmuring, it had formed monolithic bluffs, shimmering waterfalls, and soft green valleys.

The valleys were a haven and a sort of preserve for vanishing wild things, such as the mink, the smallmouth bass, and the elusive red wolf.

In the river's darker places, one could almost smell the fossils and the dampness of another time—a time eons ago when the Gulf of Mexico covered it all.

Bearded old men, one with a peg leg, memento of some war, said, "The river was named for the herds that once grazed here." They lamented that the buffalo were gone now, like so many other wild things. But the river had not been tamed, and the country along its shores was still wild, a last frontier, so to speak.

These same old men, dressed in faded overalls, used to sit on the porch of Rankin's crackerbox store—a store plastered with signs advertising 666, chill tonic, and Bull Durham tobacco. All summer they would sit outside the fly-specked screen, hoping someone would listen to their tales, their signs, and their old sayings.

Barefoot kids with a penny to spend were their best audiences. The old men told us we could see the wind if we rubbed sow's milk in our eyes. We grinned, dug our toes in the red earth, and pretended to believe everything they told us. But we were not taken in by their bit of sorcery. We could have been if they had told us something having to do with love.

Love was one magic we believed in. There had been one summer during those early years when all the conversation of the mountain folk focused on a family and its love for a child. In a way, it is a community story. And it is a story I want to tell. To do so, I will have to rely on memory, on hearsay, and on tales grown tall with time.

Chapter One

A NEW BEGINNING

The summer Rud Marshall lost his wife in childbirth and his mother with typhoid, folks discussed him a lot, particularly two old men who were close to the family.

Every day Beard Snowden, a bachelor who lived with his sister, and Af Combs, who slipped away from his wife, Sadie, would make their way to Rankin's crackerbox store. Seating themselves outside the fly-specked screen, one would let a sentence fall, then pause to see what memory it would evoke in the other. "It shore is bad about the Marshall women." Beard spoke as though he had not said the same thing yesterday; as if by saying it again it would soften the blow to the community.

Af nodded his gray head slowly, and a grimace made a half moon out of his toothless mouth. He fished in a hip pocket, brought out a snow-white handkerchief, and wiped a tobacco stain off his overall bib. "It shore is. It's bad for Paul, but Rud's more broken up than his pa. Of course, his ma was old. You expect death when a-body is old. But Lord-a-mercy, Ruth was only twenty-eight."

Beard's blue eyes were sad and questioning under his bushy brows. "You wonder about the fairness of a thing like that. To think they waited ten years for that young'un, and it didn't make it into the world."

"Rud's the kind that makes a good father. I'm judging by the way he loves wild things. He's always got something around—nurses it back to health and turns it loose." Af took out his pocketknife and picked up a piece of kindling.

"I know what you mean," Beard chuckled at his memories. With some difficulty he moved the keg so his peg leg would be in the sunshine. Then he said, "Recollect when they was payin' bounty for wolves?"

Af nodded. His eyes brightened, knowing the story that would follow. "Well, I talked Rud into trapping with me. I didn't know airy a thing about wolves. But Rud talked to the county agent. Agent said we ought to soak our traps in walnut stain. Like I said, I didn't know what I was doing. I brought along some rabbit guts for bait. Rud told me, 'That won't do. We got to use stink bait.'"

"Stink bait!" Af appeared surprised at the proper place. He asked the right question at the proper time.

"What in tarnation did you put in that stink bait?"

"Don't ask me," Beard said. "Something Rud dreamed up hisself. Smelled like a skunk, only a good deal worse. Anyway, we set our traps on Buffalo River. We covered them real good. But wolves are sharp. The grown ones didn't go near our bait. Young wolves are something else. Like kids, pups are daring, and a ky-oat blundered into one of Rud's traps."

"We lit out before light next morning. And we heard the little critter howling before we got there. Rud got all soft-hearted when he saw the little varmint. It was pretty alright—all furry like a collie. But I am here to tell you, that critter was as vigorous as a baby panther. I could no way handle him. Rud got a toe-sack over his head. He released the trap, and he carried that scoundrel home with him. You know the rest of the story."

"That I do," Af chuckled. "That was the last of Rud's trapping. He raised Old Rang from that wolf pup—the best coon dog in the county, but Rud won't even chase them."

Rud Marshall was a tall man with big hands and equally big feet. His dark brows suggested brown hair, but as it was perpetually bleached by the sun, one really couldn't tell. His blue eyes were lined from squinting at distant objects and also from observing the smallest things.

Rud was aware of his neighbors' compassion, for hill people came to sit with the sick and the dead. And they did not forget the bereavement until the bereaved had become used to carrying on alone.

When spring came, the Marshall men planted a crop as usual. But as the slower pace of fall approached, loneliness and the hard times sweeping the nation became too much for Rud. He had to get away for a while!

His decision to go was a hard one—one he hated to tell Paul Marshall. The men were cutting a winter wood supply when Rud told the old man. In the woodpile, cushioned with chips, he raised his ax, heard the block split. Making his voice sound as casual as possible, Rud said, "I talked to a drummer yesterday. Cotton's good around Helena. Pickers are gettin' fifty cents a hundred. We will need seed money next spring." Rud waited for Papa to speak. When he did not, the young man glanced across the woodpile.

Papa was sitting on a block of wood, a work-worn hand frozen to his pipe. After a while, Rud heard him say, "I hate to see you go. It's bad enough with Mary and Ruth gone. . . ."

Having no solution to the old man's loneliness, Rud raised his ax. He heard the stove wood sliver and peel away from the larger wedge. Unmindful of the fresh wood smell, he recalled some of the things that made up the person he knew Papa to be. Folks said they favored, and Rud guessed they did. Papa's features were like his, only coarsened with age and hard work.

Papa was reserved and cautious now. But he had once helped his ma float a wagon across the Mississippi by lashing logs on either side. From Batesville, where the Ozarks became wild and steep, the fourteen-year-old had guarded the wagon with a muzzle-loader while the widow woman drove to Newton County. There in the spot where Rud was working, the boy had peeled logs. With the help of Josh Sellers, their next-door neighbor, young Paul had built the first part of the dogtrot cabin they called home. He haggled the timber off their land, and he plowed around the stumps in their miniature Appalachia.

Rud's grandma was considered a well-posted woman, and she passed on her love for books to her son. When Rud was a boy, Papa built bookshelves on either side of the fireplace, where volumes entitled *Book of Knowledge* and *Wonders of the World* were kept.

But the new bookshelves and the day in the woodpile were two different worlds for Papa, and Rud heard him say, "The change will be good for you. Wish I could get away too. But somebody's got to take care of the place. Take care and be back by spring."

Rud left the next morning, taking a small bundle of work clothes. The trip to Helena was a series of walks and rides on logging trucks, wagons, and, finally, in a trembling Ford, carrying two cotton pickers. The men introduced themselves as Red and Lefty. Red was redheaded and red-freckled from working under a Texas sun. Lefty was a dark-eyed southpaw. He had picked cotton near Helena the fall before, and he knew a planter who paid more than most. "At least five cents more," the man said. "Dudley Fairbanks knows what it's like to pull a cotton sack. He inherited his plantation six years ago. Dudley sharecropped for his uncle before that."

Near Helena, the Ford left the main highway, and the road became a rutted slit in the black soil. Out of the hills for the first time, Rud took in the endless rows of cotton, the mule-drawn wagons, and now and then a black child with a string of catfish.

In the September sunset, the waist-high cotton stretched to a distant timberline. It would be dark in another hour. But the backs of the workers still dotted the fields—fields scarcely broken by the yardless "shotgun houses." Rud could see in the screenless front doors and out the back.

In the months to follow, Rud decided darkness was a mixture of hell and kindness. Nighttime brought out swarms of mosquitoes that sang you into a crazy, fighting sleep and then ate you alive. But it hid the ugliness of the gray buildings and the way the migrants lived in them. Rud shared one of the houses with Red and Lefty. The men cooked their meager meals on an oil can with a stovepipe. They slept on a pile of cotton.

Rud's employer was a new breed, one that took some getting used to. He had a soft drawl that said "heah" for here, a strange sound compared to the nasal burr of the mountain man, who pronounced the word "har." But they did have a few things in common. As Lefty said, the man had inherited his land. Like Rud, he knew the kick of a plow when it strikes a root. He knew how hard it is for a boy to stake a crow. And he knew the disheartening length of a cotton row when viewed from the end of a cotton sack.

On the short side of forty years, Dudley was soft because of the lack of hard work in recent years. Rud heard he hunted ducks with the mayor and that he campaigned for the governor. But Rud had a feeling Dudley was more at home with the field hands.

When cotton prices hit rock bottom and continued to drop, Dudley yodeled, "I'm worried now . . . but I won't be worried long." Little worry lines appeared around his eyes. But he bought himself a tan roadster, and he drove it in places where a car wasn't meant to travel. Then he parked the shiny vehicle in the field. In an expensive suit, he tramped across mud and dust with a disregard that awed the poor folks.

At the cotton scales, dangling from a propped-up wagon tongue, he sized up Rud. "Where you from, fella?"

"Newton County." Wearily, Rud hooked the corner ring of his cotton sack to the scales and wiped his sleeve across his perspiring brow. "My place is so far back we have to pipe in the sunlight," Rud kidded in mountain fashion.

Dudley's eyes took on a devilish gleam. Leaning against the wagon, his hat made a half shadow across his smooth face. Rud smelled his shaving lotion.

Rud was a proud man, and he was not unaware of the difference in their appearance. His own face wore a two-day stubble. Sweat stained his armpits. His patched jeans were nearly white with wear, and a measuring worm humped its way up his boots that were weeks past a polish.

"I passed through Newton County once," Dudley said. "Didn't care much for what I saw."

A Negro, stomping cotton down into the wagon, grinned, his mouth showing large white teeth. "Tell him about the hillbilly that lost his sow," the black employee said.

Dudley's eyes still had that devilish gleam. "May make you mad, but I'll tell it anyway. Let's see now," Dudley shifted his weight. "The way I heard it—a hillbilly went out to slop his hogs. A stern old fella, he was, and he found a sow missing. He mustered his hounds and his boys. Then he gave a blast on his huntin' horn, and his kin came a-runnin'. The old fella led them over the mountain for a feud. It seems the menfolk were shootin' out eyeballs at artillery distance, and the women and the children were throwing rocks. Then someone shouted, 'Hold yore fire. We see the old sow. She's a-reelin' in.'

"The feuders realized then the hog had not been butchered after all. She had got out, knocked someone's mash barrel over, and was sleeping it off. Still hankerin' for some kind of excitement, the patriarchs called the fightin' off, and both clans got together for a square dance and a spittin' contest."

The Negro rolled with laughter on the cotton. Dudley, with a challenging grin, waited for Rud's reaction.

Dudley's attitude raised a heat under the mountain man's collar. But he knew the exaggeration would be hard to down. Rud realized there was a frontier quality about the Newton County folk that seemed ridiculous to some of the outsiders.

That quality made them appreciate a cold-nosed hound and a true rifle. And for a goodly number, a square dance and a "chaw of tobakker" were to be enjoyed synonymously.

But Rud kept cool, mainly because he had not come to the cotton patch to defend his side of the mountain. He had come to earn a little money, and Dudley paid better than most.

Playing along with his employer, Rud laughed with the other ill-fed worker. Then sitting on his sack, he said, "I suppose you've heard about the hillbilly and his unlucky encounter with the hoop snake?"

Dudley shook his head, and the corners of his mouth curved upward with the same look of anticipation Rud had seen on the faces of Beard and other storytellers. Waving a hairy hand, Dudley said, "Fill me in, fella."

"It happened a long time ago, but it seems like yesterday," Rud began in true mountain style. "A feller, I can't remember the name, was out in the timber cuttin' firewood. While he was clearing some standing room, he uncovered a hoop snake. Now, a hoop snake is a remarkable reptile, known not only for its forked tail, but for its unusual locomotion. The man tried to kill the snake, but dropped his ax. With no other escape available, he decided to outrun the snake. But the critter tucked its tail in its mouth and rolled along in hot pursuit. All out of breath and getting more desperate by the moment, the man hid behind a tree, praying the snake would roll on by. By accident, the thing rolled into the oak tree, came apart, and it buried its tail in the oak. Experienced folks know there is no way a hoop snake can pull its tail out of things, so the woodcutter left both snake and tree to die.

"Ten years later, a hillbilly stumbled upon the tree, long dead and laying on the ground. Being too lazy to saw down a standing oak, he cut the felled tree into sections. At noon he ate his lunch there. Without thinking, he yanked off an oak splinter and picked his teeth. Naturally, the poison had permeated every fiber of that tree, and the lazy character was dead in fifteen minutes."

Rud, like others of his kind, appreciated a good story audience, and Dudley was the best. Laughing hard, he wiped his eyes on a red bandanna. Walking the space between the wagon and the cotton sack, he slapped Rud on the back. "Fella," he said, "there are certain grand-de-dah in this town that call me a show-off and a blowhorn, but I swear you got me beat."

Dudley walked to his car and was rolling up the top when Rud started back to his row. Rud felt the man's eyes on him. When he came alongside the car, he said, "Mountain man, are you a church-going person?" Rud came up short, wondering what would come out of Dudley next.

"I was at home," he said. "Never missed a service if I could help it."

Still working at the car top, Dudley said, "My church is having a big revival. Lot of folks are gettin' saved. You'd be welcome to come." With all kidding aside, the two men looked at each other, and Rud saw a sincerity on the man's face when he talked about folks being saved.

"I'll think about it," Rud promised. He would have let it go at that, had not Dudley mentioned it again on Saturday and extracted a promise from Rud to attend Sunday morning.

After breakfast on Sunday, he dressed in the best pants and shirt he could find among his shoddy, wrinkled apparel. Red and Lefty laughed themselves silly when Rud invited them to go along.

"Dudley's church?" Red laughed. "You're kidding."

When the men saw that he was not, Lefty said, "In that garb, you are going to look like a jackass on a racetrack."

They were drinking men. Leaving them with their bottle of wine, Rud walked three miles into town. He didn't blame his companions for laughing when he saw the red brick church with its hanging chandeliers and its red carpeted aisles. Feeling as out of place as the animal Lefty had mentioned, Rud took a seat in the last pew. Some of the congregation smiled, and some introduced themselves. But

Rud did not relax until the singing began. Then he forgot himself in the familiar hymns, and the preaching that followed gave him a needed lift.

When the service was over, Dudley spotted Rud. The man brought a young woman to the back pew. "This is my niece, Miss Lucy Boswell," Dudley said. "Lucy's home for the weekend. She teaches at the deaf school in Little Rock." The planter introduced his wife and other churchfolk, who offered Rud a hand and moved on. But Lucy did not hurry away.

The young woman's brown hair, pulled up in a ball of curls, came to the top of Rud's shoulder. She had almond-shaped dark eyes and a pug nose that gave her an inquisitive look that matched her personality.

"Where do you live?" she asked and then added, "I mean *really* live?"

Her eyes were so friendly and so sincerely interested that Rud forgot his cotton-patch clothes. "I come from up Jasper way. I lost my wife sometime back. I got to feelin' I had to get away."

"I understand," Lucy said. Rud wondered why the pretty woman, whom he figured to be about his own age, had not married.

Out on the church steps, Dudley joined them again. In his unexpected way, he said, "Lucy, I want you to take this fella home with you. He looks to me like he could use a decent meal."

Rud's cheeks grew hot. He started to object, but Lucy insisted. "You can help me get some medicine down a sick child I am going to visit."

Later, in the Boswell's living room, which was filled with fine old furniture, Lucy introduced Rud to her mother. A small, full-busted woman, flushed by the heat of the cookstove, Edith wiped the flour from her hands and shook hands with Rud like a man would. She was the sort of woman who seemed to carry the smell of good food with her, and Rud decided she would have been at home with his mother, talking receipts, quilt patterns, and how to get the most from a garden.

"Your daughter was kind enough to ask me home for a decent meal," Rud said. "I think she could tell I need one."

The plump, little woman looked at Lucy with affectionate pride. "It's not in Lucy to come home alone," she said. "Not too many men, you understand, but women and an awful lot of children."

"Speaking of children," Lucy cut into her mother's dialogue, "I have some medicine for Randy Brown. Could you hold dinner while we run out there?"

The older woman nodded. "It will be awhile before the dumplings are ready."

In her mother's old, but perfect sedan, Lucy drove them to a sharecropper's dilapidated hovel at the edge of town. They got out of the car and went up three spindly steps to a porch with cracks so wide Rud could see the red chickens underneath. A barefoot man with a sunken face leaned against one of the corner posts. With his brown hands cupped over a harmonica, he played, "Nobody seems to want me, or give a helping hand. . . ." He nodded but did not stop playing. His barefoot wife saw Rud and Lucy coming, and she opened the tattered screen.

In a dark corner on a rag-pile bed, Rud saw a yellow bag of bones. The boy's eyes were blank, his body covered with sores—all symptoms of pellagra's final starvation.

"We've tried jest about everything, Miz Boswell." The anxious mother twisted a filthy apron with work-worn hands. "Did you brang that medicine you was telling me about?" she asked.

"I brought it," Lucy said. She went to the zinc water-bucket, measured two teaspoons of yeast into a tin cup of water. Rud helped her pour the mixture down the struggling child. Then Lucy instructed the woman on how to give the rest of the package.

On the way back to her mother's house, Rud said, "Does that yeast really cure?"

Lucy's hands tightened angrily on the steering wheel. "Yes," she said. "But they get sick again, because the planters won't allow enough space to grow a proper diet. Until they are given a vegetable garden, drugs won't help much."

Back at her mother's place, Lucy parked the car between the white cottage and a small vegetable-flower garden. Inside they found the table set with the nicest dishes Rud had ever seen, and a casserole was steaming with chicken and dumplings.

Later, with a decent meal under his belt, Rud walked Lucy to the train station. On the way he told her about the loneliness that brought him to the delta and about his interest in wildlife. "Many species are disappearing, and only a change in man's thinking can stop the decline," he said. "I encourage folks in my neighborhood to love animals and to learn some of their interesting habits. Kids are about the only ones who really listen. Hill folks are so used to trapping and skinning, they think it's the natural thing to do."

"You are a refreshing man," she said. "I have always thought it wrong to kill for fun. That's what most men do. The way I see it, I could have been born an animal myself. You know what I mean—we have no control over our birth. When I consider the lives of man or animal, on a personal level, it makes me kinder."

"I would imagine you need a lot of kindness and understanding in your teaching job," Rud said.

Lucy nodded. "Children come to us from all over the state. Often as not, they don't know why they come or why their parents leave them. Deaf and without a vocabulary, there is no way to explain that to a six-year-old. Some are like caged animals for days after their parents leave. It is my job to earn their trust, for trust is the first step to learning."

When the train puffed into the gray station, Rud experienced a moment of panic. He had never known a woman like Lucy, and he didn't want to lose her. Ruth, his childhood sweetheart and his wife for ten years, had been a sweet, gentle person, and he had loved her in a way that belonged only to her. But now that Rud thought about it, they had never done much talking, or maybe it was more like they had never done much sharing. He had assumed men had their interests and women had theirs. It was good to be able to share thoughts with a woman who responded with ideas of her own. "Will you be coming back anyways soon?" he asked.

"Usually not," she said. "But I could if you asked me to." She raised her honest face, and the meeting of eyes triggered an extraordinary feeling within the man. It was as if he had been yanked up from a detached, limbo existence and dropped into a meaningful situation where he fitted comfortably and excitingly into place.

Rud proposed to Lucy on her return visit, and they were married during the Christmas holidays. After a small, church wedding, Lucy's mother visited a daughter in Memphis, leaving the newlyweds to honeymoon in her house. Then Lucy returned to her teaching job, because there would be no replacement for her until March.

During that time Rud worked for Dudley as a sort of straw boss, a job the man had arranged for him when cotton picking played out in November.

When March came, Rud spent half his savings on a rickety truck, as he needed it to haul Lucy's wedding gifts and other belongings to the farm. Eager to get home, Rud drove all of Saturday night so they could leave Little Rock Sunday morning.

He reached the state capital a little before sunrise. With the alluvial lands behind him, Rud could see the pine-covered foothills of the Ouachitas that faded into the southwestern dawn. Hungry for the sight of his own hills, he parked the truck in front of a brick building, overlooking the Arkansas River and a snub-nosed prominence, known as Big Rock.

He opened the truck door as the sun flashed its golden rays over the horizon, and there was Lucy, coming down the steps to meet him. Rud looked about and seeing no one, he tried for a long kiss. But Lucy's lips barely brushed his. She dragged him up the wide steps, pointing and chattering as she went, about an unknown child she had found on these very steps night before last. "The strange thing is—there was a note in his shirt pocket. It said, 'I ain't got long to live. Miz Boswell will know whats to be did with my boy.' What do you think of that?"

Before Rud could decide what he thought, she rushed on. "He is scared to death of me, but we will have to take him. You can see how I couldn't leave him. Not with me being the one responsible."

Rud tried to keep up with her conversation and her short fast steps, but she was a step ahead of him all the way to the door of her apartment. Then she stopped, opened the door, and pointed to a small figure huddled between some boxes.

At loss for words and for a real understanding of the whole situation, Rud stared while Lucy continued her one-sided dialogue. "I think he's the child of one of the cotton pickers I have helped. Or maybe he belongs to one of the sharecroppers. So many people are hard fixed nowadays that who knows?"

Still rooted to his tracks, Rud said, "Can't the kid tell you anything? He looks four or five—"

Lucy gestured helplessly. "His mama's name is Mama. His name is Corky."

Rud wasn't one to turn his back on a helpless creature. When it finally sank in that he and his bride had fallen heir to a son, he tried to pull the boy from between the moving boxes. The child screamed, yanked himself free, and crawled farther into the crevice. But Rud got a glimpse of his face before it took cover behind a tear-wet sleeve. A shock of colorless hair emphasized the jaundice-pallor of his complexion, and his eyes were whitish with a little circle of hazel. In them was the kind of terror Rud had seen in the eyes of his wolf pup! There was a stunned second before the man could speak. Then a hoarse whisper came out louder than he intended. "My God! The boy is blind!"

"That's why we have to take him," Lucy said. Then she explained the boy's affliction the way a doctor had explained it to her. "Dr. Holt, an ophthalmologist and the father of one of my pupils, examined the boy as a favor to me. He says the child has congenital cataracts. They cover the sight, and what little he sees is seen through a heavy fog."

"Is there a cure?" Rud asked.

"Dr. Holt says normal vision is out of the question. But functional vision can be restored with an operation and thick glasses. Functional vision, that's what we will have to work toward."

"What will a thing like that cost?" Rud asked the question, knowing he didn't have it, whatever the cost. But he was quietly determined that every living thing must see if at all possible.

"Far more than we have," Lucy repeated what was going on in Rud's mind. "But that isn't our immediate problem. The main thing right now is getting him over the trauma of being abandoned by his mother and helping him adjust to us."

"What about legalities?" Rud asked.

"That's taken care of." Lucy checked the dresser drawers, making certain everything was packed. "The authorities know the mother's desire that I have the child. They know where to find us should the need arise."

Wondering whether the boy was strong enough to make the trip, Rud said, "He looks sick."

"He isn't well. Borderline jaundice, the doctor said. The right diet will take care of that." Rud took Lucy's busy gathering of boxes and suitcases to mean the boy was well enough to travel. "I found him yesterday morning," she dropped her voice to a whisper. "I am sure he spent the night in that March wind. Here, if you'll pack the boxes in the truck and come back for Corky, I'll carry the suitcases. He gets hysterical when I touch him."

One by one, Rud lifted the boxes from around the sobbing child and carried them to the truck. When he came back for the boy, he spoke gently. "Come on, little fellow. We are going for a ride. Now you like to ride, don't you?" Rud got his long fingers around the boy's waist, but lifting him was like lifting the flailing, kicking wolf. His screams in the hallway brought teachers and a few of the older students out of their rooms. Everyone was expressing sympathy orally or in signs, and in spite of everyone's efforts to reassure the child, it was all Rud could do to get him inside the truck. Finally though, he got him on the torn seat, and Lucy climbed in beside him. She waved to her friends, and when the door slammed shut, Rud felt a hopeless shiver run through the small body, leaning against his own. Then he crumpled forward, a ball of heartache, and he sobbed, "Mama! Mama! Mama!"

A lump swelled up in Rud's throat. Out of the corner of his eye, he saw Lucy blot her eyes on a blue handkerchief. Knowing there was nothing they could say, they rode in silence. Corky cried until he became exhausted, and then he fell into a jerking, half-sobbing sleep.

Before they left the Arkansas River valley, Rud stopped in front of a general store. Leaving the sleeping child in the truck, the man and woman went inside. Counting out dwindling savings, Rud paid for clothes for the boy, three bottles of grape soda and some cheese and crackers to be eaten on the way, and a five-gallon can of gasoline. Then Rud turned north. On the gravel surfaced State Highway 7, they wound their way up into the mountains.

Lucy was in new territory now. The delta woman leaned forward, her eyes taking in the tumbled range of National Forest. Viewing each mile with a childlike eagerness, she said, "I declare, those clouds are playing hide-and-seek with the wind. If you don't believe me, look how the shadows keep flitting from one hill top to another."

Rud reached across the child to pat Lucy's hand. Her enthusiasm and her adjustability to any situation left no doubt in Rud's mind. Lucy would fit into his way of life as easily as a hand into a glove. He hoped Corky would fit as well. Feeling the warmth of the boy against his knee, Rud experienced a new warmth in his chest. He and Ruth had wanted a son—so much so that they had once mentioned adoption. But they heard it was next to impossible. People didn't give kids away in Arkansas.

"Funny," Rud mused, "how things turn out." Never in his wildest imaginings had he ever dreamed when he left home that he would return with a wife and a kid. It was something to be thankful for, he told himself. He knew that better than a lot of men. God, how he knew!

Alone with his grateful thoughts, Rud guided his bouncing vehicle in and out of curves for three hours before they saw a single house. The windows of that house were out, and it stared at them like two empty sockets. There was a rock fence in back and signs of a recent garden, but no evidence of a well. "I bet there is a spring around here," Rud said, turning the truck into the eroded yard.

Leaving the awakening child with Lucy, he investigated and found the water, gurgling from the hillside a few yards in back of the house. Rud came back to the truck, held his hands toward the swollen-eyed child, and Corky came into them, complaining, "I gotta potty."

Rud took him around the corner of the house, and Lucy, shivering in the sharp wind, carried the food to a protected, grassy spot near the spring. With the sounds of nesting birds chirping out their claims, the Marshalls ate their cheese and crackers. Thirst forced Corky to drink the grape soda, but he closed his eyes against the food Lucy offered him. "I hope he doesn't get sick," she said. "He wouldn't eat this morning either."

"He'll be alright," Rud said. "Wait until he sees Old Rang and Mittens, Papa's old yellow tomcat."

Though Rud had been ready to go home since November, he did not experience real homesickness until he saw the weatherbeaten logs and the greening pasture. In the gray dampness of the drizzle that overtook them in the twilight hours, Rud saw the two milk cows, their backs to the wind, and not far from them, the mules, standing close, seeking what little warmth the other might spare. Ahead, at the end of a zigzag, rail-fence lane was the house Rud called home.

The first part of the dwelling was built in the mountain style known as the "three P's" (two pens and a passage). Such a structure consisted of two separate one-room buildings set side by side and connected by a wide breezeway which was open at both ends. Additions to the rear and a three-room second story had been added later.

He stopped the truck in front of the paling yard gate. Old Rang, his coyote friend, gave a deep-throated howl, recognized his old buddy, and leaped out to greet Rud. Then Papa came down the steps, clean-shaven and wearing his best pants in honor of his new daughter-in-law. "Thank the Lord, you're back," he said. "And thank the Lord, you found someone to cook biscuits for us." He hugged Lucy, and the men shook hands, unable to show what was in their hearts, yet knowing without showing. After some small talk about the raw weather, Rud leaned forward and in a whisper, explained the thumb-sucking child that Papa would find in the truck.

The old man shook his head, unable to believe what his son was telling him. To lose the dearest person on earth was bad enough, but to be blind and not understand the loss was unthinkable. Without hesitation, Papa went to the child and opened his arms. "I want my mama," Corky whimpered.

"There, there," Papa soothed. "You are going to be alright." He slammed the car door, and with the child in his arms, he led the way up the stone steps.

In the drafty breezeway, Rud saw his mother's begonias and geraniums, dead in their lard buckets. Four cane-bottomed chairs, worn slick with use, were sitting where the women had left them. The past never lets go of a person entirely, and the chairs brought back that last summer the four of them had sat there—Mama with her quilt pieces and Ruth with the small gowns.

"Come in. Supper is about ready." Papa opened the door,

and Rud snapped back to the present. The wide-throat fireplace was piled with logs, the fire casting a cheerful glow on the braided rugs and the flower-garden quilt on the "front-room" bed. From the kitchen came the putt, putt of the old blue percolator. It added its bitter fragrance to the spicy smell of pork sausage, frying on the black stove.

Papa threw a cushion in front of the fire, and he set Corky on it. Suddenly shy, he said, "I was wondering Miss, I mean, Lucy, if you are any good at making biscuits. I do fairly well on other things, but I am a little ashamed for company to see my bread."

Half serious, half kidding, she said, "I didn't let on to Rud, but I was a little nervous on the way, thinking you might not want me in your kitchen. Thanks for needing me." Papa found an apron for her, and the two of them chattered off to the kitchen. Rud saw Mittens go curl himself in Corky's lap, the thin arms folded around the animal's purring body. Then Corky leaned forward, thumb in mouth, his pale cheek resting on the cat's fur.

When the biscuits were done, Rud carried Corky to the kitchen. When the four of them were seated around the homemade table, Papa said, "How old are you, young fellow?" To Rud's surprise, Corky laid his buttered biscuit on his plate and held up five fingers. To draw him out, Papa said, "Well what do you know; that's about the age of Old Rang." Rud grinned, knowing as Papa did, that the dog was more like six. But each figured, what's the difference when a child is all puckered up with a heartache you can't really justify.

After supper, Rud helped Lucy clean off the table. Then he led her upstairs to show her the bedrooms. "Papa sleeps downstairs. I guess you'll want the boy in the room next to us," Rud said.

Lucy nodded, her eyes taking in the high headboard which Rud's grandmother had hauled from Kentucky; the highboy with the mirror on one side, drawers on the other; and a balloon-top trunk.

"You can make any changes you want to make," Rud said. Then he added, in case Lucy was wondering about Ruth, "This has always been a company room. Don't know that I have ever slept in here."

"It wouldn't matter," she said. Then remembering something, she turned to face her husband. Putting her arms around his neck, she gave him the long, serious kiss she had brushed aside that morning.

When they came back to the fireplace, Corky was half asleep and huddled around the cat, his thumb in his mouth. Lucy tried to pick him up. "Your bedroom is next to ours," she began, but got no further. The child pulled away from her and began to scream.

"Let me see what I can do," Rud said. He picked the boy up, went to the rocker which Mary Marshall had used to rock away his hurts. Holding the child the way he remembered his mother holding him, Rud began to sing one of her songs: "Jesus loves me, this I know. . . ." Rud felt the sharp, little body relax as Corky fell asleep.

Chapter Two

THE WAYS OF MOUNTAIN FOLK

Spring came early that year. Two days after Rud came home, he was back behind his plow, contented, and feeling as though he had never been away. As he broke the thin land, the hollows echoed with the voice of one plowman and then another, geeing and hawing their mules. Peach trees in the small orchard were in full bloom, and Rud smelled the fragrance of the wild plum that grew in the fence rows. From the barn loft came the crowing of a rooster, and the hens cackled as they flew off their nests—nests where Papa gathered plump, brown eggs from sweet-smelling straw.

Spring was Rud's favorite time of year. For him it was a time of beginning anew, and, as always, he felt the year had great potential.

In his boyish enthusiasm, he made a brown paper kite. He made it for Corky the same way that Papa used to make a kite for him. And he said as Papa used to say, "We can't let all this wind go to waste. We've got to use it for something." Though the child could not see the golden speck against the cobalt sky, he felt the tug of the long twine, and his face, frozen by sadness, melted for a time. It was a great March for Rud. But in some ways, it was less than ideal for the rest of the family.

For Lucy, it was the first time she had ever filled a wash pot with well water. It was the first time she had ever tried to build an open fire in the wind, and it was the first time she had ever scrubbed overalls on a rub board. But she was a determined person, and these inconveniences were small bothers compared to Corky's emotional upsets. No matter how kind or how patiently Lucy approached the child, he drew back from her, and he became hysterical if she tried to force her will on him.

The boy went to Rud when he wanted something, and now and then he would talk to Papa. But most of the time, he was a thumb-sucking shadow, waiting for Rud to come out of the field. His daily outbursts and his screaming nightmares made life difficult, especially for Papa, who was too old to cope with twenty-four-hour confusion. To ease the tension, Rud left his plow from time to time to take his family on impromptu walks around the farm.

When Lucy insisted that he teach her to milk, a chore considered woman's work by the hillfolks, Rud took her and Corky across the greening pasture to see a newborn calf.

In the morning sunlight, they watched the yellow heifer, her tail waving as she nudged and sucked. Foam dripped from her greedy mouth, but the little animal could not hold all of the yellow milk.

"How long before we use part of it?" Lucy asked.

"Eight days," Rud said. "In the meantime, the cow has to be taken care of, or her bag will go bad. After the calf sucks, I milk what's left on the ground."

"Show me how," Lucy squatted beside her husband. The udder was slimy with slobbers, but she took hold. The jersey was an easy milker. At the first try, the woman made a small stream; then a healthy one splattered on the ground. Rud tried to include Corky as much as possible. The man reached out and drew the boy up between him and Lucy. When he did, Corky raised a timid hand. He touched the cow's satin flank, and he grinned.

Against the splatter of the milk and the ringing song of a meadowlark, they heard the sound of an ax, coming from the adjoining farm.

Turning an ear southward, Rud said, "That's Granny Sellers, chopping wood. Bet she's been off somewhere, helping with a new baby. Otherwise, she'd have been up to see us."

Rud suggested a visit with their nearest neighbor, and Lucy agreed. Walking in that direction, the man and woman keeping stride, the boy and Old Rang aways behind, Rud said, "Granny is quite a character, one you'll like. She lost her husband and a young son in the flu epidemic. Clarence was my childhood friend. He was born when Granny was past forty—like a second family, for she had married sons out in Oklahoma. They're no help to the old woman. So she's made a new life for herself as the community midwife. Though she is penniless, she accepts charity from no one beyond an occasional load of firewood."

At the edge of the pasture, Rud helped Corky over a rail fence. At a square, once-white cottage, perched on a mountain shelf between Rud's farm and Pleasant Ridge school, they saw a small, black figure, chopping wood which had been delivered in tree-limb lengths.

When Granny saw the family approaching, she dropped her ax and smoothed her black cotton in womanly pride.

"When I heerd you was back, I knew you'd be a-comin' to see me," she said, going to meet Rud.

The tall man lifted the little woman off her feet, and she pretended annoyance. "Put me down, you rascal. I want to see your boy and this pretty girl you married."

Rud introduced Lucy and the boy, and Granny, smelling of sweet snuff, hugged them both. "I love that husband of yorn like a son," she told Lucy. "Loved his mama like my own daughter, too."

Gathering up an armload of wood, she led the company inside. Dropping the wood in a box, she said, "You folks sit and make yoreself welcome. I'm goin' to chunk up this fire. The sun's warm, but the wind and the house is cold."

Shivering in a blue sweater and a blue print dress, Lucy pulled a black rocker up close to the iron stove. Granny opened the door, stirred the ashes from the red embers, laid in some pine knots, then some oak. When the pine caught fire, Granny closed the door, and her bright eyes turned on Corky. He stood beside Rud, his white hair windblown, the bib of his overalls, bearing Old Rang's muddy paw marks. His left hand clung to Rud's knee, the right thumb in his mouth. Granny pushed a sawed-off nail keg with a cushion top toward him. "Sit on this footstool, little fellow. I'll get you a couple of chocolates before you leave."

Corky smiled shyly around his thumb, and Granny told Rud, "He looks awful peaked to me. Soak some rusty nails and give him the water. The iron will put color in his pale cheeks."

Rud liked to tease the old lady. Knowing she expected him to do so, he said, "Nail soup isn't too bad, son. But some of her concoctions throw the stomach into a real tizzy."

Grinning a toothless smile at her well-known joke, Granny said, "I admit, the powdered lining of a chicken gizzard would be pretty hard going down. That's why I try other teas first." She reached into her apron pocket, brought out a can of sweet snuff and a blackgum twig, chewed to a soft pulp. Dipping her "toothbrush" in the powdered tobacco, she told Lucy, "Sometimes children balk at my usual remedies. Then I tell 'em: 'I will pour my stronger medicine down you,' meaning the powdered lining of a chicken gizzard! I don't have a speck of trouble with them after that."

Though Granny was no physician, her little black bag, containing calomel, senna, epsom salts, and dozens of her own herbs, was a reassuring sight in the community. Whether her medications did any good or not, she was a great help to a family during any kind of illness, and especially during a woman's confinement.

Looking as fragile as a last year's dandelion, she could be seen coming. With snow-white hair in a crown of braids and dressed in an ankle-length, black dress, she looked even tinier than her ninety pounds. She would arrive a few days before a woman "came down," and she stayed until the baby was nine days old (the required rest for a mountain delivery). During that time Granny cooked, washed on a scrub board, and doctored the older children. Her pay was money "once in a coon's age," and the rest of the time the pay came in the form of eggs, potatoes, or a side of meat. "Things I ain't got time to raise myself," she said.

While Rud and the old woman talked, Lucy's eyes took in the room—the ancient clock on the stand table; the long, black gun on hooks above the front door; a weather calendar on the peeling, white-washed walls; and a spray of peach blossoms in a fruit jar on the fireboard of the closed-in fireplace. "Where you been?" Rud asked. "I knew you weren't home or you'd 'a' been by."

"I been over on Pigeon Roost Mountain. Man and his wife both down with malaria. I took care of the kids."

"Pigeon Roost is some of the roughest terrain in this county," Rud told Lucy, "And it's all of fifteen miles. Knowing this woman, she walked all the way there and back."

"It ain't as bad as it sounds," she said. "I spend the night with friends along the way. I'm always welcome, and I'm grateful for the rest."

Rud did not say so, but he knew many of her nights were an experience rather than a rest. Most of the families were large in that area, and they lived in crowded quarters. Almost always, Granny had to sleep with a child, often one that wet the bed. When an embarrassed mother apologized, Granny said, "That's nothing to be plagued about. I been wet on by half the folks in these hills." Then she left the bed-wetter some corn silk tea and hurried on her way.

Knowing malaria was a health problem throughout Arkansas, and especially in the delta country, Lucy said, "Have you found a cure for fever and chills?"

The old woman shook her head. "I been trying to. Folks can't hardly afford quinine. Most are so hard up. Peach tree tea, boneset and fodder tea, helps, but it don't cure. They got that problem where you come from?"

"Much worse, because there are so many swamps," Lucy said.

"Then you know what I am up against. It don't seem to be but one cure for malaria, and like I said, a lot of folks don't have the money to buy quinine."

Though Rud kidded Granny, he had no doubt but what many of her remedies saved lives. Living in an area where there were no all-weather roads and the nearest doctor was fourteen miles away, Granny applied hot mush poultices to blood poison. If that didn't work, she soaked the wound in hot salt water or hot vinegar.

She brought "risins," or boils, to a head with a piece of fat meat, a little crushed potato, or a piece of bread soaked in sweet milk. These remedies caused a painful, pulling sensation, and they did the job.

She used coal oil, or kerosene, as did all the mountain people, on fresh wounds, such as a nail puncture, cuts, and snake bite. Like most of her neighbors, she applied wet tobacco to insect bites, stings, and snakebite if coal oil wasn't handy.

But Rud knew her teas best, and kidding her again, he said, "Granny carries some beautiful-sounding herbs in that little black bag, such as golden seal, yellow puccoon, and butterfly weed. But when she came to doctor me, she always brewed up a pot of galling peach tree tea, or worse yet, a puckery fluid made from persimmon bark."

"You must 'a' had summer complaint," she said, "Ain't nothing better than persimmon bark for 'running off,' but the bark has to be scraped upward, on the north side of the tree." Turning her mischievous eyes on Lucy, the old woman continued, "Herbs ain't all I carry in that black bag. Ask any kid under ten, and they'll tell you I carry babies. If that rascal keeps poking fun at me, I'll drop one on the Marshall steps!"

"I'd prefer persimmon tea," Rud laughed with the women. But he knew he spoke the truth.

Granny treated "pneumony fever" with blistering mustard plasters. Sometimes when she found a willing victim, she rubbed the chest with a paste of lard and chicken manure.

A number of Granny's patients refused her more outlandish, but supposedly more effective, cures. Rud smiled, remembering when Sam Rankin had the mumps. Granny wanted to tie a string, soaked in hog manure, around the storekeeper's waist. "That'll keep 'em from going down," Granny said.

Shaking his swollen head, Sam said, "The mumps might not go down, but my wife most certainly would. She would go downstairs to another bedroom."

"Well, I think it's time this boy gets his chocolates," Granny's raspy voice cut into Rud's memory of laughter around the store. The old woman went to a black trunk and raised the balloon top. She brought two pointed candies to Corky and three quilt tops for Lucy's inspection. While the young woman was admiring them, Granny said, "Choose one. That roughneck you married is mighty dear to me. One of these days I'll get a quilting party started. The church folk tries to get a quilt ready for all the newlyweds. Rud being what he is in this community, they'll want to do something nice for you."

Unable to choose, Lucy closed her eyes and said, "Eeny, meany, miney, moe." Then she pointed to a wedding ring pattern. When Granny laid it in her lap, Lucy leaned forward and kissed the woman's weathered cheek. Sputtering happily, Granny said, "I ain't no ways as good at quilt makin' as I once was. My hands are bunged up with rheumatism. About the best ointment I know for that ailment is a salve made from skunk oil, and I lost the 'receet' years ago. I lost the receet for my best blood stopper, too."

Rud knew Granny's blood stoppers depended on the afflicted area. Soot and cobwebs were pressed into a cut or puncture, but nosebleed was treated by letting blood drip on hot ashes. Rud considered the latter treatment a strange one, but the strangest of all her cures was the one she used on "liver-growed" babies. "Tell Lucy about that disease I'm always joshing you about," Rud said.

"He means liver-growed. Ever hear of the ailment?" Granny asked.

"I don't believe so, but I am interested," Lucy said.

"Liver-growed means the liver has got attached to one of the baby's vital organs." Granny got to her feet and turned off the damper on the stove. When she sat down, she said, "A child can't grow right until the liver is free. To break it a-loose, I pull the left hand and the right foot back until they touch. The harder it is to do, the worse the liver is growed. Though Rud don't believe in the sickness or the cure, I can show you dozens of women who will tell you their babies didn't grow right until they got the treatment."

Knowing it was a popular belief, Rud said, "I'll vouch for that."

Though Granny tried her hand at all kinds of doctoring, she was first of all a midwife. If an unborn child was carried high, she predicted a girl, while a low lump indicated a boy. "That's just simple arithmetic," she said. "Boys weigh more as a rule, and they drop faster. I don't miss many times," she told Lucy. Then turning to Rud, she said, "You remember the Worth family that joined the church before you left?"

Rud nodded. "A young couple and their little girl. Seemed like fine people."

"None better," Granny said. "I mention them because I want to tell Lucy something funny about their little girl. When Sarry got in the family way, Ben wanted a boy because they already had little Rose Ann. When Sarry came down, they called me, naturally, and it was a boy. Ben showed Rose

Ann the baby, and he said, 'I guess we'll have to name him after Granny. After all, she's the one that brought him.'

"A few days later, someone in church asked the little girl what they named her baby brother. She said, 'Clifton Eugene, but we plan to call him Granny.'"

Rud and Lucy laughed with her, and Corky, with a ring of chocolate around his mouth, giggled.

"It's things like that and my caring for the kids that makes my work worthwhile," Granny said. "When you are alone, it's good to be included in family life, even though it's not your kin. The kids, the little rascals, bring home a lot of old sayings they think was invented yesterday. Same ones you and Clarence used to repeat, and of course, me and your mama heard them in our day."

Rud knew what she was talking about. There were hundreds of cures kids passed from one to the other, cures no one believed, but kept alive by telling. Smiling, he said, "You mean:

Sty, sty, come off my eye,
Catch the first man that passes by.

or:

Wart, wart, come off my hand,
Go back to the frog from where you came."

Granny nodded. "That's the ones. And you know others like, 'bury a bean leaf and tell no one,' and 'hide a dishrag if you really want to get shed of warts.'"

"When a boy lost a baby tooth, a gold one would grow in if you didn't lick the cavity," Rud said. "But a tush would grow in it if a hog stepped on it."

"I know where some of the stuff comes from," Granny said. "Beard Snowden and Af Combs. I have heard them two tell kids they could see the wind if they rubbed sow's milk in their eyes. And a girl would change to a boy if she kissed her elbow. But according to them old codgers, a kid's nature depends on the day the child was born."

Laughing, Rud and the old woman repeated together:

"Monday's child is fair of face.
Tuesday's child is full of grace.
Wednesday's child has love to show.
Thursday's child is full of woe.
Friday's child is kind and forgiving,
Saturday's child must work for a living.
But the child that is born on the Lord's day,
Is a special child, and he'll know how to pray."

Rud got to his feet then, and Lucy, with the quilt in her arms, did likewise. At the door, Granny hugged Corky goodbye. Then she tipped his chin up, and Rud thought she was examining the child's eyes. If she was, she saw something more disturbing. "This is a Thursday child if ever I saw one," she said. "Give him some willow bark tea. It calms a person. It'll make him sleep better."

Knowing Rud questioned many of Granny's medicines, Lucy looked at her husband. Nodding, he said, "I hadn't thought about it, but willow bark does seem to calm. We'll get some on the way home. There are trees all along the river."

When they left Granny, Rud detoured by way of the Buffalo. Three hundred yards from his back door, a cow path slanted down from the pasture to the river. A spring-fed creek trinkled from the bluff above the trail. Across the river was a narrow valley. "The best land we own," Rud told Lucy. "I am thinking about an acre of cotton in that bottom. Hill people don't raise cotton the way they used to. It sucks the land, and the boll weevil won't leave it alone. But we need a money crop if Corky's going to be able to see."

Rud looked around for the boy. He and Old Rang were having a tussle between the river and the house.

"Wait here," Rud told his wife. Leaving her at the top of

the slope, he made his way down to the water's edge. On a narrow sandbar, a willow tree angled across the river, its roots piled with debris; its drooping boughs made little eddies in the crystal stream. Breaking off some of the twigs nearest to shore, Rud said, "I hope this will help the boy. I have read there is something in willow bark that soothes like aspirin."

Corky was still out of hearing range when Rud joined Lucy. The woman slipped her small hand into her husband's large one. Headed toward the boy and the tumbling, yellow dog, she said, "It seems like we have had the boy forever. It's funny how a child enters your life, a perfect stranger, and a week later, you can't remember what life was like without him."

"I know what you mean," Rud said. "And I been thinking we ought to name him. Oh, we'll probably go on calling him Corky, but it would look funny on a man's records. You have to think ahead when you got a kid."

"There's the question of a birthday, too," Lucy said. "Birthdays are important to children." Ahead of them, they watched Corky stumbling in his efforts to keep up with Old Rang, who had lost interest in the boy and was sniffing each clump of grass for a cottontail.

"How much do you suppose he sees?" Rud asked.

"Not much, according to Dr. Holt. A foggy image up close. Nothing at a distance." A puzzled note crept into Lucy's voice. She said, "Each day he seems less afraid of everything and everybody except me. I wonder what it is about me that upsets him so."

Rud put his arm about Lucy's shoulders. He knew how hard she was trying to fill the void in the little boy's life. And he had only one answer for the child's attitude toward her. "It was a mighty scary thing being left out in the dark all night. It will take time for him to get over that."

"I know that. But it's something else. Something to do with his mother. If only he would talk about her; tell us something about himself."

"He will come around. But we will have to wait until he is ready. In the meantime, what about Sunday School tomorrow? Think the kids might be good for him?" Rud asked.

"It won't hurt to find out," Lucy said.

Chapter Three

CHIPPER JOINS THE FAMILY

Sunday was a bright day in which wind, bird, and frog teamed up in an earth-awakening song. Lucy, in a pink wrapper, was frying bacon when Rud came downstairs. He poured himself a cup of coffee and measured a spoon of sugar. Then he said, "Guess what! Corky tells me he has been to Sunday School. Said the kids sang, 'Let it shine, let it shine.'"

"Did he say where?"

Rud shook his head. "I told him about the church, about the children he would meet and the songs they would sing. Then Corky said, 'I know. I went to Sunday School once. The kids sang, "Let it shine, let it shine, let it shine."'

"'What was the name of the church?' I asked, casual like. He shrugged. 'What was the teacher's name?' I tried again. But he put his thumb in his mouth, and he walked away."

"Not much, but something," Lucy said. She put breakfast on the table. Papa came in from feeding the mules.

Complaining of feeling poorly, he washed at a side table, containing a cedar water bucket, and a white wash pan. Then the family gathered around the bacon and eggs.

Later, when the milking was done and the chickens fed, the Marshalls, including Papa, walked down the mountain to Pleasant Ridge. The half mile was so steep and rocky that even if there had been money for gasoline, Rud would not have driven the truck. Mountain people were used to walking. With the sun warm on their backs and the sounds of spring all about, the distance seemed short.

The A-shaped, white building with six windows on either side, was set in a little meadow, between two bluffs. On one side there was a cemetery with brown stone markers; on the other side, a well-worn path led to a spring out back. Rud often wondered why the school-church was not called Pleasant Valley or Pleasant Hollow, but Pleasant Ridge it was, and it was good to be back with salt-of-the-earth folk, such as Af, Beard, the Rankins, and other families that greeted them on the steps.

Inside the building, school desks served as pews. The pulpit stood on the stage of the "big room," or the room where the four upper grades were taught.

Two old women, with their gray hair tightly coiled and a trace of snuff at the corners of their mouths, held out a work-worn hand to Lucy. Rud introduced Sadie Combs, and Jessie Fife, Beard's sister. Florie Hawks, a simple blonde with a baby on her hip, said, "We been hearin' 'bout your kid. What in the world would make a no-good woman run off and leave a blind kid?"

In spite of the woman's ignorance, anger rose in Rud's chest. He looked down at the child, wishing he could protect him from the blows that were bound to come. He saw Corky's pale eyes drop from the woman's face. His thumb went into his mouth, and his nose pointed at the floor.

Not bothering to answer Florie, Rud pushed Lucy to the front of the room. "I want you to meet our pastor," he said.

In front of the handmade pulpit, the man introduced his

family to Preacher Adams, a farmer pastor who "preached right out of his head." That was the best kind of preaching, according to mountain folk, who believed, "Called preachers don't have to fiddle with notes."

Preacher Adams greeted them with a firm handshake. "Glad to have you back," he told Rud. "Looks like you got yourself a fine family. Bottom country must 'a' been good to you."

Like everyone else, the preacher was barely making ends meet, and a tired, imploring expression masked his dark face. His ancient blue serge suit had not shrunk with hard times the way the man had, and it looked as though it had been thrown on a scarecrow. But Rud, like most of the community, appreciated the man's labors. He worked hard in his own rocky fields, and even harder in the Lord's. "Looks like we are goin' to have a good gathering," he said, and his dark eyes took on a youthful sparkle.

Lucy sat down in one of the pews, and Rud led Corky back through "the little room," to the cloak room, just inside the back door. A group of boys from six to twelve were meeting inside. Rud looked around, expecting to see Esther Brown, the boys' teacher and a woman whom Rud considered the finest in the country.

"Miz Brown had to leave sudden for Oklahomy," towheaded Bobby Rankin said. "She told Billy Higs to tell Preacher Adams. But Billy decided to teach us hisself."

Rud had never seen Billy in church before. His ma had died when the youth was a baby. His pa, a wild kind of man who hunted for a living, never came to meetin'. That being the case, Rud couldn't imagine the sullen teenager teaching anything except a hound. But he had heard about Billy getting saved, and Rud with his soft heart hated to hurt the new convert's feelings.

Still uncertain, the man introduced Corky to some of the boys. Then Bobby Rankin said, "Don't worry, Mr. Marshall. I'll look after the little kid." Rud convinced himself that he mustn't be overprotective. Releasing Corky's hold on his pant leg, he sat the thumb-sucker between the young protector and the loud-mouth teacher.

From what the children said, and later from what Corky told him, Rud was able to piece together the following scene:

While the adults were singing "Bringing in the Sheaves" in the opening exercise, Billy began a Bible story about Joseph. For orneriness, two of the older boys said, "We're thirsty. We're goin' to the spring."

"Yo're not leavin' this room!" Billy's pimpled face was determined. But the boys leaped out an open window.

Billy's backless Bible fell on the floor. "Come back har. Come back or I'll bash your bloomin' heads," he shouted.

One of the boys came back and taunted, "Billy Higs on his daddy's knee. He looks like a bullfrog on the root of a tree."

"You heathen! I'll get you for that!" Billy shouted. As the agitators hoped, he climbed out the window and gave chase. The rest of the boys refereed the race.

In the confusion, Corky began to cry, but no one noticed. The child wandered out of the room and out the back door. Still sobbing, he went around the side of the building, stumbled into the rocky road, and started back up the mountain.

When the child got to the house, he turned the doorknob and went inside. Silence told him he was alone. More frightened than ever, he went back to the porch, sat on the top step, and sobbed.

Wiping his nose on his sleeve, he heard Old Rang bark. He went down the steps, around the house, and across the pasture. The dog saw him coming and stopped his endless search for a rabbit. When Corky caught up, the dog went down the slope and crossed the river.

Corky sat down and edged himself down to the narrow sandbar. The river was shallow there, but swift as it poured down smooth brown stones into a wide deep pool. Old Rang yelped on the bluffs beyond the valley, but Corky did not try to cross the river. He lay down on his stomach, put his hand in the stream, and fished the clear water for a stone that might interest him. Suddenly he felt the riverbed move. Like something rising from the dead, he saw with his foggy vision a ghostlike bullfrog free itself from the bottom.

The frog climbed aboard a platform of grass and sticks. Though Corky could not see the frog's true color, the sunlight glistened on its greenish sides. He saw its throat swell out like a gray balloon. It went "Barrrumm! Barrrumm!"

The sound surprised Corky. "Silly frog," he said. Then there was a splash, a sprinkle on Corky's nose, and the frog was gone.

After the splash the boy lay still. When the river rushed on without interest, he raised himself on an elbow. Corky wondered what to do next. He listened for Old Rang, but he heard nothing except the rising wind.

The hickory above his head groaned. Corky felt a torrent of air sweep over the water. Then something coldly soft, plopped on his forehead.

The child bounced to his feet. Squatting he ran his fingers over the sand. Then he picked up a cold, hairless animal that was no larger than a man's thumb.

Corky cupped his hand to protect the tiny creature from the wind. He felt the quiver of a leg. A weak heartbeat throbbed against his palm.

Needing both hands to pull himself up the steep incline, the boy put the baby in his jacket pocket. He had started up the slope when he heard Rud call his name.

The man had a feeling the child had gone home. He circled the house, while Lucy looked around the barn. When Old Rang barked from across the river, they looked in that direction, and there was Corky, his white head topping the hill.

Lucy, ahead of her husband to begin with, reached the child first. She threw her arms about him, crooning, "We heard what happened. And the whole church is out looking for you."

Corky stiffened at her touch, and when Rud reached him, he pushed her away. Digging in his pocket, he held the tiny animal for Rud to see.

The man's blue eyes squinted. Then getting down on the boy's level, he said, "What do you know! You've found a baby squirrel!"

"A squirrel!" Lucy's voice was as eager as a child's. "I have never seen a baby squirrel before," she said.

Rud laughed. "I imagine that goes for most folks. Where did you find him?"

Before Corky could answer, Lucy said, "We will have to know, so we can take him back to his mama."

Corky's fingers closed over the animal. He backed off a couple of steps and became hysterical. "His mama's gone," he screamed. "His mama's gone. Mama! Mama!" he repeated over and over.

"In that case, we will have to take care of the little feller," Rud said. Seeing the helpless look in Lucy's dark eyes, he lifted the child and the squirrel and carried them to the house.

Papa, along with Beard, Af, and Sam Rankin, met them at the backyard gate. When Rud had found the boy missing at the close of Sunday School, Preacher Adams had dismissed the congregation, and everyone was out looking for the child.

When Sam saw Corky was alright, he said, "I'll go tell folks he's been found." The heavyset young man left then. But Af and Beard followed the Marshalls into the house, asking each other, "What made the fool kid think he could handle a gang of boys?"

"It's my fault," Rud said. "I should have known better than to leave them."

"No, it ain't," Beard insisted. "In the first place, he didn't give the preacher Esther's message. Just went in there and tried to run things hisself. That kid is as hare-brained as his pa used to be."

"That he is," Af took up the dialogue. "Frank Higs was

seventeen when he married Calley—about the age of Billy—and you wouldn't believe some of the things he done." The old man paused, bit off a chew of tobacco and worked it back into his mouth.

Beard pulled a rocker alongside Rud, who was down on the floor with Corky. With one eye on the squirrel the bearded man said, "Calley was a good woman. Things would have been different for Billy if she had lived. But like you said, that Frank was unbelievable, fearless as they come, but unbelievable. I recollect one time right after they got married, Calley was down at the spring washin'. All a-sudden she heard a panther squalling on the bluff right above the wash pot. The girl left her rub board and ran to the house. Frank took his gun down there, and shore enough there was its tracks, but he couldn't find the panther.

"Figuring he might need some help, Frank sounded an alarm on his huntin' horn. Pretty soon a half-dozen men showed up with dogs barkin' in all directions. I was among them, you understand, and every time that thing would squall, the hair on the back of my neck would stand right straight up. But that Frank didn't have sense enough to be scared. About sundown, his funny-looking bulldog (the thing had one eye missing) treed the thing. Higs broke into a run, and he got a bead on it before the rest of us got there. When he fired, the panther fell over on a limb, and Higs assumed it was dead. He kicked off his brogues, and he says, 'That's my panther; I'm a-goin' up and fetch her.'"

Papa, sitting alongside Beard, chuckled. "Why didn't you go up after her?" he kidded.

"I wasn't wantin' her," Beard said. "But thanks to that fool Higs, I got her right on top of me. Knocked me to the ground, that panther did, and it revived when it landed. Of all the squalling and cussing, you've never heard the like. Naturally we men were so concerned with saving our lives we let the cat get away.

"Nothing would do, but what we keep on hunting. 'Folks won't be safe with a wounded panther on the prowl,' Frank said. About midnight we heard it screaming in a cave. The cave went down about twenty feet. Then it curved back under the side of the mountain. I figured it was a lost cause and suggested we go home. But Higs yanked a grapevine out of a tree, and I watched with my mouth hanging open while he tied the vine around his ankles. 'Let me down in thar,' he said. With a gun in one hand and a torch in the other, he went down in that cave, head first. The thing screamed, the awfullest sound you ever heard, but Frank laughed his crazy, fearless laugh. 'I see him! The light's shining in his eyes!' he said. He fired one shot. Then we hauled him up, clinging like a madman to his panther."

Papa fell back in his rocker, his body shaking with laughter. When he could speak, he said, "A funny thing happened to me and Billy last summer. The government had just finished them dipping vats for Pleasant Ridge. It was the hottest day in August when it came time for this community to drive our cattle down and rid them of ticks. As if the heat wasn't torture enough, I walked two miles on a stone in my shoe. When we reached the dipping vats, I sat down on a stump, and I had just got my shoe off when Billy came up with his pa's herd.

"'What you aiming to do, Mr. Marshall?' he asked, seeing my shoe off. I don't know what got into me," Papa said. "But I decided to josh him a bit. I said, 'I aim to take a bath. That stuff kills chiggers. And it looks like it might cool a fellow off.'

"That kid gave a crazy laugh, and before I could blink my eyes, in he went."

Af had heard the story before, but he never tired of a good joke. He laughed so hard that tobacco juice sprayed his whiskery chin. Beard had missed other tellings, and he found the vintage joke so funny that he slapped his peg leg and did not feel the pain until his laughter subsided.

Throughout the storytelling, Rud was sitting cross-legged on the floor, trying to decide what to do with the squirrel. But he was aware of the old men's laughter, and it kindled a forgotten warmth in his chest. It was like old times, having the three of them together on a Sunday afternoon.

Lucy had gone upstairs to change into a housedress. When she came back, she asked Rud what she could do to help him. "Bring me a warm, smoothing iron," he said. Her heels clicked into the kitchen. When she came back, she had an iron, wrapped in a tea towel.

Rud took some quilt scraps out of a shoe box that he found on the sewing machine treadle. He put the warm iron inside, and laid the squirrel on top of the towel. The warmth put new life in the tiny body. Her legs kicked, and she made little mewing sounds. "She'll need warm milk and some kind of a feeder," Rud said, wondering what he might use. "I'll take care of it," Lucy said, her heels clicking back into the kitchen.

The old men had leaned forward, watching quietly. When Lucy left, they sat back again, taking up their conversation about the Higs; a subject which Rud had not realized could be so interesting.

"Have you seen that hound what follows Billy around?" Beard asked.

"I've seen him. He's so poor you can't see his shadow," Af said.

"You mean he's so poor you can't hear him trot on dry leaves," Papa chuckled.

"He's both of them, and he's hungry besides," Beard went on. "I know because I was up at their cabin a few weeks back. Me and Frank was sittin' on the porch beside five gallons of slop—that is, if you can call clear dishwater with two white biscuits slop. Anyway, we was a-sittin' there, and that red hound kept lapping that water, trying to get them biscuits. I guess it was like dunking for apples, because he drank all the slop before he got 'em. If that wasn't a sight for the buzzards! He looked just like a sawhorse in a family way. He was a-slushin' around the porch, looking for something else to get into when Frank saw a kitten on the table. 'Throw that cat out here. He's a-lickin' in the gravy bowl,' Frank told Billy.

"Billy picked it up and tossed it out, easy like. But that hound caught that kitten in midair. And I mean to tell you, he swallowed it whole."

"The devil, you say!" Af was so flabbergasted that he couldn't think of a story that would begin to compete with that one. He was glad when Lucy came back to the room.

The woman had fashioned a nursing bottle from a small perfume bottle and a round of oilcloth. A drawstring held the cloth to the bottle, and the center, pulled to a sharp point, had a darning-needle puncture.

Rud forced a drop of milk through the hole and worked at the squirrel's mouth. He saw Corky's lips open and close in his eagerness to have the animal eat. The old men leaned forward again, begging the pink creature to open its mouth. "For the boy's sake," Beard said, "for he's had enough sadness already."

At last the mouth opened, but the milk poured out the corners, and the squirrel struggled against Rud's hand. "You're killing it," Corky screamed. Then its tongue pulled and repulled, and the animal was sucking.

"That's a squirrel," Beard said. "Just look at her suck!"

"You mean she is eating?" Corky asked, uncertain.

"Of course, she's eatin'!" Af ruffled Corky's hair in an affectionate gesture. When the boy smiled, Beard lifted him to his bony lap.

The men watched the squirrel suck until her stomach was full. Then she rolled herself into a pink ball and was perfectly still.

"She's asleep now," Beard told the child. Then he went on to say, "I hope you can raise the animal. A squirrel is a happy, talkative creature."

"I don't know that I would tell the kid a squirrel can talk," Af corrected his friend.

"Why not?" Beard defended the statement. "I don't mean English. But squirrels have got their own way of talking. What do you think they use that bushy tail for?"

"I ain't thought much about it," Af said.

"Then I'll tell you. A squirrel talks with its tail. Oh, it uses the tail for other things, too, like a blanket in winter. But the tail is used aright smart in squirrel language."

"I'll go along with that," Rud backed Beard up. "A scared squirrel will drop its tail and run. But a brave one will fluff its tail to make itself look bigger. Then he will scold and chatter from a tree limb."

"Believe it or not, a squirrel can sing," Beard said, feeling the boy's excitement. "They got a morning song that's happy and chattery. Then they got a love song that's so soft an inexperienced ear would take it for the whimpering of a mouse."

Papa, leaning back in his rocker, took in all the comments. Then he said, "Squirrels have got a lot of instinct. Animals with instinct know how to build a house and what food to eat without being told. Casting an affectionate eye toward Lucy, he said, "You don't need school teachers when you got instinct."

"That is right," Lucy came back. "But since men haven't been overly endowed with it, they need school teachers—if for nothing else, to cook their biscuits. And I think it's about time I stirred some up."

When Lucy called the menfolk to dinner, Corky took off his lightweight jacket and he laid it over the baby squirrel.

Then they gathered around the kitchen table. Papa asked Af to bless the food. After the old man asked God's blessings on the food, he said, "Thank ye, Lord, for an excitin' day, for it's such things and the warm friendship of these good people that makes an old man's life worth living." From that day, the men stopped by regularly to see Corky and the squirrel.

Chapter Four

LEARNING ABOUT SQUIRRELS AND FARMING

The Marshalls learned a lot about squirrels in the following weeks. Until Chipper (so named by Corky) was ten days old, she demanded day and night feedings. Nature had her on a three-hour schedule, and she chattered in her shoe box until one of them came to feed her. When she was ten days old, a grayish fuzz appeared on her pink body. At three weeks she was covered with short reddish hair. Like a human baby, Chipper crawled first, pushing herself forward with her hind feet. Tiny teeth showed through her gums. But her eyes did not open until she was six weeks old. Once she saw the world around her, the shoe box was a daytime bed only. When night came, she crawled down into the curve of Corky's body.

Like a tightly closed bud opening slowly to a spring sun, Corky opened to the caring of the baby squirrel. Though he was too young for full responsibility, Chipper claimed him as her parent from the time he placed his jacket over the shoe box. If one of them forgot to put the covering back, the little animal would whimper until Corky picked her up or until the familiar garment was spread over her.

Though Corky was still shy around Lucy, only saying what was necessary to her, he had a number of timid questions for Rud. One day he said, "Why does Chipper like me better than you?"

At the time Rud and Lucy were each milking a cow. The boy was sitting on the trough between the jerseys, holding the squirrel. Rud's tanned face crinkled with laughter. "The little scamp loves you like you were his daddy. She loves you the way I hope you love me and—" Rud hesitated, looking at Lucy, "the way I hope you love me and your mama."

An incredible sadness clouded the child's face. He held the pet on eye level, looked into its face, and then said, "My mama's gone."

Rud felt a deep pity for the child and also for Lucy. The woman had tried to find her way into Corky's heart. When they stood up, their milk pails in hand, she motioned that he was to ignore the comment. Rud said, "Getting back to your question. Squirrel's have a keen sense of smell; all wild animals do. No doubt she recognizes you and feels secure under your jacket, because the smell means safety, and food—things a mother squirrel gives."

A gentle rain had fallen the night before, and from the looks of the sky, more would come. When Rud turned the cows into the pasture, he told Lucy, "It's too wet for breaking land. I think I'll take Corky fishing. We might get a couple of bass for dinner."

Corky let out a squeal of pleasure. When Lucy started to the house, a pail of milk in each hand, he put Chipper in the woman's apron pocket.

Rud took a shovel from the tool house. They dug some red worms from beneath a manure pile. Then they crossed the pasture, and Rud helped Corky down the slope.

"River's up," he said, digging around in the can for a worm. He selected a long one, broke it, baited both hooks, and cast them into the deep pool. Just below the hickory where Chipper was found, Rud patted a rock big enough for the two of them, and they both sat down.

Old Rang had followed them and was hunting on the bluffs beyond. The sound of his bark, a distant cowbell, and the damp smell of last year's leaves, created a special mood for Rud. He loved rainy days. As he saw it, rain created a beauty too shy to come out in the sun. Colors sprang out in the moss, leaves, and bark that were too low-keyed to be appreciated in the sun. Trees seemed to bunch up in rich clusters, and the sound of dripping leaves cloaked him in a muted privacy that was good for sorting thoughts. The strip of bottom land was broke and harrowed. Cotton had not been planted there for a good many years. It might make a bale. A bale would "my-nigh" pay for the boy's operation. It would sure be good to have a strip of delta soil. But God forbid that he would have to live in that flat country. Rud was satisfied that a fellow wasn't likely to find a prettier place than his own farm.

That meant a lot to a person even though he barely made a living.

Deeply content, Rud took in the beautiful scene about him. Thumbnail leaves painted the hills pale green. Violets nodded in earthy leaves, and frogs croaked their throaty songs between showers.

Corky turned his serious little face upward. Pointing, he said, "Back there, I saw a frog. I saw it just before I found Chipper. Is he still down there?"

"Must be," Rud said. "Probably one of the basses in that frog band. Listen!"

The boy listened, and Rud began to conduct. "Hear the cellos—zonk, zonk, zonk. Now the kettle drums—barrrrummm, barrrrummm—and the piccolos trilling beenk, beenk, bureenk. On second thought, that may be your frog going waah, waah, waah on his big bassoon."

Corky threw back his head and laughed. Then they were quiet, each content with his pole, until a falling twig caused Rud to look up. Up the hickory trunk, about twenty-five feet, and almost level with a rocky shelf that overhung the hill, was the hole from which Chipper had fallen.

Rud motioned Corky to quietness. He staked their poles. Then Rud helped the boy up the incline through a tangle of vines to the rocky shelf. As the tree was growing on the sandbar, when Rud sat down, the hole was on eye level about twelve feet away. The hole was about six inches across and so shallow that Rud could see why Chipper had rolled from it. The shallowness made the vine enclosure a ringside seat to the activity going on in the squirrel's nest. "See them?" Corky whispered, his hand trembling with excitement.

Three squirrel noses poked through the opening. "Yes," Rud whispered. "I can see them. There's plenty of room for all three to see out, but they are acting like children. They are pushing and shoving and nipping each other for the best spot."

Corky's body shook with laughter at the imagined scene. But Rud's hand quieted his giggles. Mother Squirrel was coming home by way of the treetops. "That's to keep other animals from knowing she has young in this tree," he told the child.

Throughout the journey across elm, cottonwood, and oak, the old squirrel was a tightrope walker with her tail acting as a balance. She entered the hickory, came down the trunk and into the hole. The babies began to whimper and tumbled about in search of a nipple. "I hear them," Corky whispered. Then they settled down to filling their stomachs.

When the squirrel children were full, the mother cleaned their fur, pausing to look nervously about, for she sensed the presence of humans. Instinct told her the babies must be cleaned, and while she was licking one, the other two tried to clean themselves. They licked their undersides and then fell over sideways, trying to get to their own backs. "They are acting just like Chipper," Rud said.

When the babies were cleaned to the mother's satisfaction, she poked her nose out of the hole and started her roundabout descent.

At the river's edge, she drank, then smelled the ground in hurried, nervous sniffs. She found the place where a hickory nut was buried, dug into the damp earth, and lifted out a nut. While Rud was explaining the squirrel's storehouse to Corky, she sat back on her haunches and cut away the hull. Then she hurried to another spot and dug again. This time the nut was sprouted. A tender mini-tree was seen on top of the black shell, and a webbing of root hung below. The animal put the seedling back in the hole; then she patted the earth, as though she knew she was planting a tree.

The meal finished, she washed herself. Then she disappeared into the undergrowth.

The adventure over, Rud helped Corky back to the trail. "Wait here while I collect the fishing poles," he said.

But Corky went into a tantrum. "I don't want to go to the house now," he screamed.

Rud got his poles, and he had to half carry the boy halfway across the pasture. Suddenly a flutter of wings startled the screaming child, and Rud caught sight of two birds in flight. One was shiny black with a white vest; the other was buff brown with dark stripes. "That was a pair of bobolinks," Rud said, trying to pacify the child. "Stop your bawling, and we'll look for their nest."

A few steps off the trail at the base of some Johnson grass, Rud found the nest. It was set in an earthy bowl and was anchored to the grass roots. "I want you to see the straw roof that protects the eggs from rain," Rud told the boy. Corky rushed forward with outstretched hands. "Hold on," Rud said. "Let me get a couple sticks. The birds won't sit on the nest if it has been touched by human hands." Rud parted the grass with the two sticks. Inside the opening he could see all three eggs. One was reddish, one white, and the other one was gray. "Normal colors for a bobolink," Rud said. "These birds do farmers a service," he continued. "Pick up your pole, and I'll tell you about them."

Sniffing, Corky picked up his pole. As they walked, Rud said, "At first, the young are fed entirely on insects. That cuts down on harmful bugs that destroy our crops. The male bird guards his family against intruders. He sounds an alarm if danger comes. Listen! That bobolink call is part of his wild, varied singing. Sometimes he sings in flight. When he does, the air is filled with a rich melody.

"I like the bobolink song," Corky said, wiping his tears on his sleeve.

"So do I," Rud answered. "The bobolink song is a good plantin' sign—best I know for plantin' corn." Rud opened the back gate and leaned the poles against the paling fence.

Like most of his neighbors, the mountain man waited for certain bird calls, the position of the moon, and other signs before he planted certain crops.

Replanting corn that failed to come up was considered children's work. For this task youngsters were given an apron full of corn and a hoe for replanting the skips. To insure work instead of play, children were told they must not laugh or shout, as noise would cause the corn to rot in the ground. Rud remembered that after a few hot rounds in the field, he had once planted his "turn" of seed in a hollow log. Papa wondered why the replants didn't come up, until he discovered a million stalks growing from the log.

When Rud told Lucy the story around the dinner table, Papa said, "You were luckier than the girl that sliced the cabbage." Chuckling, he said, "Feller told his kid daughter to deworm some cabbage. In a fit of anger, she sliced each head right down the middle. When the old man discovered the mischief, he decided to trick a confession out of the girl. He took a quarter from his pocket and he said, 'I got two-bits for the kid that will slice all the cabbage.'

"The gal snatched the money from his hand. Grinning from ear to ear, she said, 'This quarter belongs to me, cuz I dun done it.'

"'Yo're durn right, you dun done it!' shouted the old man."

Setting a hen was considered a woman's task, and Lucy was interested in it. She planned to raise a large flock of laying hens. Eggs were traded for groceries and kerosene at the store. Those who wanted cash could load their eggs on a truck that came through the community once a week. Lucy planned to buy what clothes they could afford with the egg money. She told herself that this would be her contribution to the family.

To start the project, Papa showed her how to sort a setting of eggs. According to her father-in-law, a long, rough egg would produce a rooster. A round, smooth one would produce a pullet. "And eggs must not be set when the wind is from the south. Eggs set in a south wind just won't hatch," he said.

Papa helped Lucy sort the eggs at the kitchen table. As they talked, a rooster crowed at the back door. Corky called Chipper, and then he went slowly up the stairs to search for her. "Got a pencil?" the old man asked.

Lucy dug a cedar stub out of a little wicker basket which contained a black whetstone (for sharpening knives), some loose matches, and a yellow chunk of beeswax. She sharpened the "penny pencil," and the old man marked the eggs.

"All hens time their laying with the settin' hen. This way, we'll know the fresh ones," he said.

Before they went outside, Papa told Lucy to mark the date. She marked April 2 on the big calender advertising Dr. Jayne's Expectorant, a tonic that was supposed to cure everything from loss of hair to whooping cough. She wrote: "setting hens."

Then she dropped the stubby pencil back in the basket. Papa picked up the sunbonnet, containing two settings of eggs, and the back screen slammed behind them.

With the April sun warm on their backs, Papa said, "Takes twenty-one days for eggs to incubate. Do all your setting in the next few days. May chickens are no good. When the weather gets hot, young chickens sleep themselves to death."

Lucy questioned some of Papa's signs, but she was aware

that he, like other mountain people, had figured out a crude, yet workable science for getting the most out of his farm. She knew that newcomers, drawn to the area by cheap land, often laughed at their backwoodsy methods. But few of them survived, and those who did soon learned to incorporate some of the old ways in with the new.

Because she was willing to learn, Papa explained why he did things. To repel insects, he used a cedar post to hold the hen nest, and he used cedar poles for chicken roosts. "Cedar helps keep down mites," he said. "So do cedar branches." He mixed red peppers in the chicken feed to make the hens lay. "Makes them eat good and they drink a lot more water," he said. He tied kerosene strings around the chickens' necks if they looked "croupy," and he tied corn shucks to the leg of a clucking hen to discourage setting.

When Lucy questioned him about a muleshoe, nailed above the hen house door, the old man chuckled. "I don't put no stock in it, but there's an old sayin' that a muleshoe will keep the hawks away. Then, too, it's supposed to bring luck, and heaven knows we can use some of that."

The Marshalls, like other Ozark farmers, did not believe all the signs and sayings popular in the area. Each farmer lived by a few, experimented with a few more (just in case), and the rest were quoted in jest.

There were a number of things women were not supposed to do. Bread was supposed to be broken, as cut bread was bad luck. Different hands in a cake would spoil the batter, and "strange hands skeers lye soap," they said.

Though Papa knew of no one who took the lesser signs and sayings seriously, deep down, most of the old-timers believed unusual bird or animal behavior could be a warning.

One evening when the family was gathered on the front porch, the talk turned to unusual happenings. Papa said, "I have never seen anything that couldn't be accounted for, though once I thought I did. After I'd taken a girl home from a pie supper, I was walking home from away over close to

Low Gap. In a steep place with bluffs all around, I was kinda skeered. There was no moon, and it was an awful dark night. I was walking along a path, no road or nothing, and all a-sudden, two lumbering, snortin' things tore loose in front of me. I darn near died of heart failure. As if the commotion wasn't enough, I saw two white heads running ahead of me. Well, I had on a tight pair of shoes that squeaked when I walked. I don't know what they did when I ran, cuz I warn't listening.

"Next day, I talked Beard into going over there with me. Just wanted to clear it up in my mind. If it was a hant, I wanted to know it. If it warn't, I wanted to know that, too.

"When we reached the spot, Beard began to laugh. There on the bluff above us, two black sows, white from the shoulders up, were rooting in the leaves. I have been skeered by other things like that. But there was always a reason. I can't say as much for Mary, Rud's mother. She saw unaccountable things. Maybe she believed and looked for 'em. I don't know. But I'll tell you what happened a long time ago. . . ." Papa paused, collecting his thoughts.

It was an exceptionally hot night for the first of May, and the family had retired to the cane-bottom chairs, hoping to catch the breezeway draft. Lightning streaked the west, and there was a low rumble of thunder.

"Looks like rain," Papa said.

"Whippoorwills outdoing themselves is a good sign," Rud added.

Then Papa went on with his story. "Like I said, this happened a long time ago. Before Rud was born, we had another boy then, called Mark. One day I went to Jasper and didn't get back until after dark. Mary, with the baby on her hip, went out on the porch and was listening for the sound of my wagon. All a-sudden a whippoorwill flew out of the woods, and it lit on the baby's head. Mary knocked it off. But the thing flew down three times. Then it perched itself on the roof, saying, 'Whippoorwill, Whippoorwill, Whippoorwill.' Then it flew away. Mary was all upset when I came home. 'That's a shy bird, not one to fool around with human beings. I got a feeling something bad is going to happen,' she said.

"I kidded her out of it, and we forgot the bird before we went to bed. That night Mark took diphtheria. He died three days later. May have been coincidence. I don't know about such things. She told me the same thing summer before last, when she saw a redbird tapping on her window. Well . . . you know how she died with typhoid."

"I have heard similar stories from my mother," Lucy said. "She thinks cats can smell death."

"I don't think—I know they can!" Papa said. "I have sat up with a corpse when there were half a dozen cats, squalling on the window screens. Was enough to make the hair stand right up on a feller's neck."

Rud listened to their talk. As the thunder rumbled closer, he ruffled Lucy's hair, and kidding her he said, "I'm going to tell you what I know to be a truth. If a screech owl calls and you answer it back, the owl's liable to come down the chimney, scatter the fire, and burn the house down."

"Pshaw," Papa laughed. "There are hundreds of them old sayings. They don't mean a thing. I'm glad Rud likes to write down facts about animals. There's a lot to learn. Ought to be more folks studyin' wild things. They are goin' to die out if someone don't take notice."

A flash of lightning lit up the breezeway. In the minutes before the sound of rain was heard, Rud said, "I have started a log on the squirrel family. I figure the boy will learn from observing them. It's helped him—having Chipper and making them trips to the ledge—I know that much already."

"I know it too," Lucy said, getting quickly to her feet. When the rain hit the shingles, she led her menfolk into the house.

Chapter Five

MAKING NEW FRIENDS

Springtime was a lean time for most of the hill people. Cured pork, canned vegetables, and dried fruits had a way of playing out a few weeks before garden stuff came in. Wild greens were a welcome relief from hominy and dried beans. Since wild greens were eaten throughout the South, Lucy also enjoyed them with her family. But she was no authority on which ones were eatable. "Any plant a cow will eat is good for human consumption," Rud said.

Lucy came back, "I don't know any more about cow food than I do about wild greens." So Rud tied his team to a fence post, left his plow, and took his wife and son on a greens gathering.

Poke, sour dock, lamb's-quarter, and spider's claw grew in abundance in richer spots along the river. The milk bucket was soon filled, but Rud made any outing an adventure. "There is a cooper spring up the mountain aways," he said. "The water flows over a flat rock, and there are three footprints, or petroglyphs, as scientists call such carvings."

Lucy was immediately interested, but she felt guilty about keeping her husband from his work. "Shouldn't you be plowing?" she asked.

Rud mopped his brow on a blue bandanna. "Hottest part of the day," he said. "I'll plow later in the evening and make up."

After the steep climb, Lucy was surprised to find the spring in use. A rock milk house was built around the flat stone, and the crystal water flowed through troughs where there were covered crocks ladened with thick cream. On the mountain shelf above, there was a log cabin, surrounded by a well-swept yard. "That's Esther Brown's place," Rud said. "I hear she's home from Oklahoma. She'll be back in church next Sunday. Be teaching Corky's class."

"Good. I'll be glad to turn it over to her," Lucy said. She had been teaching the boys since Bill Higs' failure.

"I want you to meet Esther before we leave here," Rud said. He opened the milk house door wider and pointed down. A strip of sunlight fell across three footprints, as smooth as one would expect if they had been set in wet cement. "My mother was one of the first settlers in here," Rud said. "Papa was a boy, but he remembers Indians coming from Oklahoma to drink this water. They believed it could restore health. I think the petroglyphs had something to do with it, because there was a legend the old Chief told about some phenomena that brought the spring into being.

While Lucy was examining the prints, he took a gourd dipper off a nail by the door. Starting with Corky, they drank in turn. When they left, Rud hooked the door. Lucy's eyes took in a flower-scented corner of Esther Brown's backyard. Blue iris and pink roses were nodding about two brown stones that looked like the marking of a grave. "Is that a grave?" she asked.

"I'm afraid so," Rud said. He wiped his mouth on the back of his hand. A yellow cat rose from the grass, stretched, then walked over, and curled itself about Corky, who had dropped into grassy shade.

Hanging the dipper back on the nail, Rud said, "These hills are full of drama. And I dare say, there is none more poignant than the story of Esther's son."

"You mean her son is buried in the backyard?" Lucy's eyes were wide with curiosity.

"I see I'll have to tell you about it before we raise Esther," Rud said. His calloused fingers reached for the bucket of greens. Lucy called Corky to his feet. With the yellow cat following, they started a slow walk up the incline.

"Fifteen years ago, Widow Brown and her son passed our house in a rickety wagon, pulled by two white jennies," Rud began. "The little vehicle was piled high with living plunder. A cow, a bull calf, and a three-legged dog, called Cripple Dick, followed on ropes.

"Mama and Papa insisted I go calling with 'em, saying I should invite the young man to church. When we got here, we couldn't believe our eyes. That old cabin was as bright as the hills in springtime. Esther has a way of dollin' a place up. You'll see what I mean, potted plants and do-dads made up of everything. But that's not what impressed me. It was the paintings! I had never seen real art before. While Mama was admiring the woman's tea cakes and gettin' the receipt, I was moonin' over the pretty pictures. They were leaning here and there all over the place.

"'My son Neal is an artist,' Esther said. 'And so was his father. That's where Neal's talent came from.'"

"Then there was a step on the front porch, and we were introduced to a dark-eyed, frail-looking young man. He had a canvas under his arm. Neal was a likable person, one you get to know right off. He showed us the canvas, a newly painted redbud tree. The tree was leaning against gray cliff rocks, and the pink flowers were so real you could almost smell them.

"'Two of his father's paintings are hanging in the Smithsonian Institute,' Esther said, her round face beaming with pride.

"'He had a year of study in Paris. Then his health broke. A

St. Louis man, he came to Eureka Springs to be around some artist he knew, and also he hoped the mountain air would be good for consumption. He wasn't well the whole time I knew him, but he lived until Neal was fourteen. We met at an art fair and were married soon afterwards. Neal learned to paint about the time he learned to walk,' she said.

"The young man's fame spread fast," Rud said. "Young folks went to the cabin to have their picture painted. They paid whatever they could, and Neal saved every cent, planning to go to New York or some such place. But it was another talent of his that won the respect of the menfolk, a talent he inherited from Esther. He knew how to farm. With his ma's help, Neal cleared a little strip of bottom land, and he raised a bale of cotton to the acre and more potatoes than anyone in these parts. This led the men to predict a brighter future in farming than he was likely to see as an artist. But Esther saw potatoes and cotton as stepping-stones to the fame and honor due to her son.

"According to Mama, all the young women were in love with Neal. And in spite of Esther's ambitions for her son, she longed for a daughter and grandchildren. Knowing this, Neal told Mama, 'Some day I'll get married and have a half a dozen kids, but right now all my time is taken up with painting.' Then flexing his fingers, he had fear in his voice. 'If only that old rheumatism will lay off when cold weather comes,' he said.

"After hot August, folks around here welcomed the cool weather and the mist that veiled the mountain tops. But it laid Neal up with a stiffness in his joints. At that time, the state had no funds for maintaining roadways, and once a year all men were summoned under penalty of arrest to do a certain amount of work. When the summons came to Esther's cabin, Neal was laid up and didn't report to work. A few days later the sheriff came to escort him to the county seat.

"Ordinarily the arrest would have meant no more than a night in jail or extra days on the road. But a gang of drunks was thrown in the cell with him. And having nothing better to do, they made Neal their victim.

"'Let's have kangaroo court,' one suggested. After some imitations of trying Neal, the largest bully said, 'I sentence this fancy pants to be my servant for as long as we are confined to this jail.' Throwing Neal a handkerchief, he said, 'Clean my boots.'

"When Neal made no effort to do so, he was grabbed by the collar and thrown on the floor. Amid the shouts and encouragements from the other youths, the bully kicked Neal in the stomach. The young man struggled to his feet, and he knocked the bully to the cell floor. His tormentor came at him again, and this time he advanced with an open knife. Down the two crashed, snarling and clawing like two animals. Finally there was a cry of pain.

"The drunk staggered to his feet, stood for a dazed second, then fell forward. His own knife was plunged to the handle between his shoulders. Neal had won in the battle for his life! But he was twelve miles from home, and the mountain people from one neighborhood didn't take kindly to folks from another. With five cell-mates against him, Neal was sentenced to ten years in the State Penitentiary.

"Folks around here were stunned by the injustice of it," Rud said. "Neal was a frail, gentle person. We knew he had been pushed into a death struggle, or he'd never have fought.

"Everything Esther could sell was sold to save her boy. She didn't have much. There had been too many years with a sick husband. When winter came, she was penniless and didn't have a pair of shoes. The church took up a collection, and folks who didn't claim to be religious brought the preacher money. He took it to the woman. There was nothing any of us could do to ease the pain of Neal's letters. He wrote telling her the damp cell was making him helpless with rheumatism.

"Down to the state capital Esther walked. It took her three days to make the trip on foot. She talked to the governor, and he was sympathetic. He advised Esther to get up a petition, signed by everyone who was willing to testify to Neal's good character. With old Cripple Dick, she became a familiar sight, trudging from farm to farm, gathering signatures. Finally she dispatched it to Little Rock, but justice worked slowly. When Neal was released two years later, he had to be carried to the depot on a stretcher.

"Tenderly, Esther put her son aboard. Handing the conductor one ticket, she said, 'I'll be walking back. A neighbor will meet him in Russellville with a wagon.' The conductor had heard of the woman and was sympathetic. Pushing her down beside her son, he counted out the fare from his own pocket.

"Esther tried to restore her son's health, but she fought a losing battle. I think he had TB, same as his dad," Rud said. "Anyway, he died with some kind of bad coughing right after he got home. For reasons of her own, Esther buried him in her back yard. Maybe she feels she is still looking after him. . . . A person can't tell what goes on in a human heart."

When Rud opened the back gate, he saw Lucy wipe a tear from her cheek. "It happened a long time ago," he comforted her. "And Esther isn't one to hold a grudge. You'll see what I mean, and you'll see the paintings."

When they reached the sagging front porch, a plump woman in a blue checkered starch-crisp dress opened the screen door. In spite of Rud's consoling, Lucy expected a sad, embittered woman, but nothing could have been further from the truth. Her brown eyes were merry, and she laughed at herself a lot. "Come in," she said. "I was just gettin' ready to play my Graphophone. Maybe the boy will want to listen to it while we talk." Laughing, she said, "I got this little portable selling Cloverine salve. One record came with it. Times have been so hard I ain't had a chance to buy another." She wound up the machine, put the needle in place, and Gene Austin began to sing, "Just Mollie and me . . . and baby makes three. . . ." Grinning, Corky sat down on the floor in front of the machine. Esther filled his hands with cookies. Then she focused all her attention on Lucy. "So, you're a teacher. Are you going to do any teaching around here?" She pushed two rockers toward her guests and took a cane-bottomed, straight chair for herself.

"I'm hoping to, when Corky starts school," Lucy said.

"Mountain people have great respect for teachers," Esther told her. Rud had told Lucy the same thing. She felt she had been accepted by most, in spite of the soft drawl that marked her as an outsider.

"I thank you for teaching my Sunday School class," Esther said. "I was plagued my-nigh to death when I heard what a disgraceful thing that Bill Higs pulled. Of course I blame myself more than I do the boy. I shouldn't have sent word by Billy, knowing he's been raised by a pa that ain't got too much sense. His mama was a good woman, but she died with pneumonia some years back. The boy ain't had no book learning or any other kind of training since."

Neal's paintings were still on the walls, but Esther didn't mention her son.

"Looks like you've got a nice mess of poke," she said, eyeing the green shoots protruding from the rim of the bucket. Rud had set it by the door.

"There's more than enough for us. Won't you take some?" Lucy offered.

Esther shook her head. "I've got plenty left over from what I picked yesterday. But much obliged. Poke is my favorite greens."

"Mine, too," Rud sandwiched his comment between the women's chitchat. Then getting to his feet, he said, "I've got a lot of plowing to do between now and dark." Lucy agreed that they must go. Corky got up from the floor.

On the way to the door, Esther laid a hand on the boy's shoulder. "I heard about your squirrel," she said. "I love wild things. Half the time I got something in the box behind the cookstove. Usually it's a bird that's fallen from its nest, or some animal that's been hurt in a trap. Things like that are a lot of company. Besides, it gives me something to do. I'll be down to see your pet," she promised.

When they were out of hearing range, Rud said, "Esther don't need anything to do. She plows like a man, raises corn, potatoes, garden stuff, and chickens to sell for things she has to buy. Like the rest of us, Esther's hard up, but it's worse for a woman alone. Even so, she teaches her SundaySchool class, pieces quilts for folks in·distress, and she has a handout for anyone in need."

The Sunday school teacher lived up to her promise to visit Corky. And for Chipper, it was love at first sight. When Corky introduced his pet to the woman, the little animal leaped out of his hand, crept around the back of Esther's chair, and then eyed her from the top of the stand table.

"Leave her be," Esther told the boy. "She is gettin' acquainted in her own squirrel way." They watched the little animal, with her thin fur and stringy tail, scurry up the stairs. Near the top, something frightened her. Down the steps she flew, landing in the middle of Mittens. The old cat woke from a deep sleep. Looking ruffled and disgruntled, he walked stiff-legged to a braided rug in front of the fireplace. There he curled himself for another nap.

Chipper hopped upon Esther's lap, sniffed the starch in her pink cotton, and then flattened herself for a nap.

Esther dropped in regularly after that. With Af and Beard also coming by occasionally, Corky was slowly coming out of himself. But Rud and Lucy were both concerned about the extreme shyness that kept the child from entering into games or any child activities with others. The shyness kept him from attracting any friends of his own age.

Esther tried to integrate Corky into the Sunday School class, but she could only take him so far. "Children can be awfully cruel," she told Lucy. "One Sunday I heard that little Hawks girl say, 'Is it true your mama just went off and left you?' I called her aside and talked to her about it. The next Sunday, right in my own class, Bobby Rankins said, 'What makes your eyes look so funny?' Unable to answer questions like that, Corky spends most of his time in his seat, sucking his thumb."

Rud gave the problem a lot of thought, and one Sunday he got an idea. Lucy was combing Corky's pale hair, getting him ready for Sunday School when Rud appeared in the doorway. Wearing a shaving-cream beard, he said, "I've been thinking, the boys and girls would get a kick out of watching Chipper suck her bottle. How about it? Want to show them, Corky?"

Rud watched the boy draw into himself. His thumb went into his mouth, and he mumbled, "You can show 'em. The kids don't like me."

"Then you have to make them like you," Rud said. He finished his shaving. Then he went to the barn. When he came back, he had a dusty cage that had once been the home of a pet coon.

Lucy got the Bibles and a bottle for Chipper. Corky was still uncommitted, but on the way there, he said, "I didn't feed Chipper anything. If she is real hungry, she won't jump out of my hands. She'll be too interested in the bottle."

At the door of the classroom, Rud put his arm about the boy, and he could feel Corky's heart pounding. He wanted to stay and help him, but decided the shyness would not disappear as long as the boy clung to him.

Rud gave him the cage. Lucy gave him the bottle. Just then Jean Hawks saw the little squirrel, and she let out an excited squeal. "Kids," she yelled, "come see what Corky's got."

Youngsters of all ages gathered around, oh-ing and ah-ing. Then they asked questions, questions that Corky did not shrink from. "This is her bottle. If you will let me sit down, I'll show you how to feed her."

Esther, watching it all, relinquished her teaching chair. The children helped him get situated. Corky opened the cage, took the tiny bottle from his shirt pocket, and held it up. Up on her hind feet Chipper came, grasped the bottle with her handlike paws, and began to suck.

"Is Chipper a boy or a girl?" Jean asked.

"What else does she eat?" Bobby wanted to know.

Feeling important, Corky forgot his shyness. Answering their questions the way Rud answered him, Corky told them how the baby squirrel rolled from her mother's nest. "It wasn't the mother's fault," he said. "Sometimes mothers can't help what happens." Then he told about the bits of nuts and the cabbage leaves she was taking along with the bottle. By that time Chipper had finished the milk and was trying to get away from him. Corky put her back in the cage and covered it with his jacket. "I'm covering her up, so she won't whimper during the story," Corky said. Then he took his seat beside another boy.

When the girls followed their teacher to another part of the building, Esther praised Corky for a fine job of sharing. Then she told the class the story of Moses—how the mother left Moses in the rushes, knowing the princess would find him and take good care of him.

When the handbell rang, dismissing Sunday School, the woman closed with the usual question, "Are there any questions one of you would like to ask?"

Most of her question was lost in the rush to the door. But once the boys were gone and the noise subsided, Esther saw Corky's hand was up. "I have a question," he said.

She closed her Bible and leaned toward him. "That shows you were really listening. Now what is it you want to know?" she asked.

Shy again, Corky half mumbled, half whispered, "Why did that woman leave her little boy?"

Aware of the inner tickings of her pupils, the teacher sensed the question was much more personal than it would have been if it had come from one of the other children. She breathed a silent prayer for the right answer; then she said, "She left her little boy because she loved him. The mother couldn't keep him, so she left him with a kind woman who would love him as she did."

"My mama left me," the child quavered. "It was dark, and I couldn't see. She told me to wait. I was going to wait, but that woman made me get lost!" Tears welled up in the pale eyes. His voice carried all the longing in the world when he said, "I wish she didn't make me get lost!"

"Dear God," Esther whispered. Then Rud came through the doorway. Motioning the man to her side, she asked the child if it was alright if she shared his question with Daddy.

Corky wiped his eyes on his sleeve. He nodded his head. When Esther repeated the question, Rud said: "That explains his anger toward Lucy. Now we have something to work with. Together, Rud and the teacher helped the child understand that his mama was sick. Knowing she could not take care of him, she did what Moses' mother did. She put her little boy where a kind woman would find him—a woman that loved him.

Eager for clues pertaining to the child's background, figuring they would be asked when they got around to adopting Corky, Rud said, "Where did you live?"

The boy began to sob again, but he said, "We lived by the cotton patch, but not in that first house. We lived in that other house."

"How did you get to the school steps where Lucy found you?" Rud went on.

"We walked a long way. It got dark, and I was hungry. Mama told me to wait. I didn't see where she went," the voice quavered again.

"What was Mama's name?" Rud persisted. The child gave the question some thought, decided Rud was teasing him, and his lips curved in a tearful grin.

"I done told you. I told you her name was Mama!" he said.

Rud did not press the subject further. In time Corky might remember something else. It no longer seemed important to the man. He felt the important thing had been settled. Understanding why his mother gave him away would free Corky of distrust and bitterness toward Lucy. Rud took Corky's hand. When they joined Lucy in the preaching service, Rud whispered a prayer of thanksgiving. He was certain things were going to run more smoothly now.

"Let's sing 'Praise God from whom all blessings flow,'" Preacher Adams said. He began the hymn, and Rud joined in with gusto.

The afternoon following Sunday dinner was as bright as a sunbeam, and a lazy atmosphere prevailed. Papa turned a porch chair upside down, propped a cushion on the chair back, and then stretched himself on the breezeway floor.

Lucy stacked the dinner dishes in a pan and reached for a steaming teakettle, but Rud begged her to wash the dishes later. "It's too nice to be inside," he said. "Let's take a walk and see how the crops are doing."

Lucy laid her apron on the corner of the table. She picked up a sunbonnet from the seat of a chair and put it on her head. When the back door slammed behind them, a white brood hen with twelve yellow balls scattered, clucking and peeping.

Corky, dressed only in blue overalls, left the crooked spoon he was digging with, called Old Rang, and followed his parents. The yellow dog bounded around the house, his white-tipped tail waving like a flag.

Rud opened the back gate. The boy and the dog passed through, but Lucy stepped to one side and shooed two hens from their dusting place under a clump of pink and red hollyhocks. A bumblebee left one of the pink cups and buzzed around her head. Ignoring the insect, she said, "I wish those chickens would sun themselves outside the yard."

She followed Rud through the narrow gate. He put a ring from a wagon hub over two posts, and the gate held. They crossed the south pasture to the field that lay next to Granny Seller's yard. Leaning on the gray rails of the zigzag fence, Rud looked at his corn, two feet tall, and he heard the green blades crackling with new growth. "It's looking good," he said. And the hope that burned anew each growing season flamed in his chest.

When they tired of corn watching, they retraced their steps back past the house and then walked north to the slope that went down to the river. From the top of the hill, they could see the skimpy lines of green where only half the valentine-shaped leaves of the cotton plants had come up. "Cotton is a dry-weather crop," Rud said hopefully. "Maybe it will come up yet."

The blond man, a head taller than his dark wife, stood there until Corky caught up with them. Perspiration and mud streaked the boy's forehead, and his neck had a string of dirt beads. Without any debate, Rud said, "By heck, we're going swimming!"

"You mean it?" Corky asked, not quite believing him.

"Sure," Rud said. "We'll cool off. Then we'll show Mama the squirrels."

"Ain't she going to cool off?" Corky hesitated, seeming to want Lucy to join them.

"Isn't she going to cool off," she said, the teacher coming out in the woman. But she quickly added, "She most certainly is. Wouldn't miss it for the world."

Pleased, yet a little uncertain, the boy unfastened one gallus and then let the other fall. His pug nose had a sprinkle of freckles, and his face was getting round. His pink shoulders had a white galluses cross between the blades. His swimming trunks were his drawers.

Rud stripped to his BVD's and held out his hand. He helped Corky down the path and into the rushing water. Lucy followed, barefoot. When she waded in, her housedress billowed on top of the water. Rud left Corky and Lucy in the shallow water, and he dived into the deep pool, below the rapids. In the waist-deep water, Lucy's housedress clung to her body, but the rushing water felt good.

"I wish I could swim," Corky whined, hearing Rud's seal-like maneuvering.

"Then I will teach you," Lucy said. "But we will have to go down to the still water. Here, I'll carry you. The rocks are pretty sharp." For the first time, the child held out his arms to her.

When the family tired of the stream, they made their way to the rocky shelf to look at the young squirrels. Corky was certain that the animals knew them by now, and Rud agreed. The old squirrel did not seem jittery the way she once had, and the young ones stared at them with black-bead eyes.

Lucy, in her wet dress, hugged her knees on the rock surface. Rud squatted beside her, and Corky, wearing his overalls over his wet drawers, sandwiched himself between his parents.

Hearing the people, the young squirrels in the nest began pushing and shoving, first one nose and then another poking out.

"Where is the mother?"Lucy asked.

Rud shook his head. While they waited, a yellow-vested meadowlark, feeding on insects in a rotten log, raised his black head. The bird filled the woodland with a ringing melody, but Rud did not look down. Above the bird song, his ears caught the pitter of falling twigs. "There," he whispered and pointed up.

The hickory trunk divided into three great limbs up near the top. There in the fork, the old squirrel was ripping off leaves, chewing them, and then dabbing them into a green leaf ball.

After a time, the babies began to whimper. The mother started down the tree. "She is going to feed them," Rud told Lucy. But the animal hurried on past the nest to the forest floor. She picked up a stick, carried it up the tree, and worked it into the mass. Six times the squirrel repeated the process. Then she struggled up the tree with a ball of gray moss. After she patted it down, she scurried to the whimpering youngsters.

With her mouth, the animal picked up a baby. The little squirrel wrapped its tail about the mother's neck, and the female moved swiftly up the tree.

Rud told Corky what was taking place, and the child was anxious. "Is she going to eat the baby?" he asked.

"No," Rud reassured him. "She is moving her family to a larger home."

The man and woman watched the squirrel make four trips

to the nest. The third trip took twice as long, and it was obvious the mother was tired. The fourth trip was to make certain no one was left behind. Finding the nest empty, the mother flattened herself on a limb. Her pink tongue hung out like a panting puppy. "The show's over, and it's time to go," Rud said.

The Marshall's left the tired squirrel. Damply cool in their wet clothes, they started toward the house. The sun dropped below the mountain. Before they reached the back gate, the dark shadow of the house reached beyond the yard fence, and a breeze rippled the grass where the jersey cows were waiting to be milked.

When Rud opened the back door, he heard Beard talking to Papa on the front porch. After Rud changed into dry clothes, he joined his elders. Beard asked, "How're them wild squirrels doing?" Chipper was scampering around the old man's feet, and every now and then he paused in his tales and reached down to stroke the little animal.

"They're doing fine. Old one moved her young today," Rud said. "I figure she is getting them away from fleas or other vermin."

"Could be," the old man said. Then turning his eyes toward Papa, he asked, "Do you know how a fox gets shed of fleas?"

"Can't say that I do," Papa said.

"I ain't ever seen it done, but I got it from good, reliable sources. According to these here fellers, a fleabitten fox gets a piece of wood in his mouth, and he wades into a stream of water. As the water comes up his body, the vermin begin to climb, because fleas hate to get wet. First they hop on his back. Then they hop on his head. When there's nowhere else to go, they jump on the piece of wood. The old fox ducks down then, and he swims away, leaving the out-smarted vermin on the piece of wood."

"That's one I ain't been educated to," Papa said. "But I'll tell you what I do know—fox odor changes when a female's carrying young."

"You can believe it," Beard said. "Hound can't no ways track her during that time."

"I guess it's God's way of protecting the unborn or something like that," Papa said.

Rud knew from experience that both ideas were false. But he wasn't one to try to change the older generation. He heard the rattle of the milk pails, and he left the old men to their way of thinking.

After supper Beard walked down the mountain with the family to listen to Sunday night preaching.

Chapter Six

DECORATION DAY

The last Sunday in May was Decoration Day at Pleasant Ridge. A community reunion was held in the school yard. In some ways folks looked forward to this social event more than any other. After regular church, dinner was eaten on the grounds. Then there was special singing, special preaching, and visiting with old neighbors who had moved away, but returned each year to decorate the graves of their dead.

Weeks before the event, women saved their egg money to buy new shoes and other new clothing for the family. In the hills, Decoration Day was the equivalent of the Easter parade held elsewhere.

The big day began early on the Marshall farm. When the rising sun sent its golden rays through the kitchen window, they were saying grace over their biscuits and gravy. When breakfast was over, Lucy washed and stacked the dishes in the kitchen safe. Then she hurried toward the barn with two milk pails. She had something special to tell Rud, something so special that she felt a quivery kind of joy each time she thought about it.

Half conscious of the world outside herself, she saw Papa and Corky throwing table scraps to the chickens. Clyde, a turkey gobbler which Papa had raised in Rud's absence from the farm, gobbled a sedate march toward the bread, while the less dignified hens raced past the gobbler, cackling and squawking.

Rud had driven the cows up from the pasture and was putting them in the stalls when Lucy joined him. She watched him throw some cane heads into the troughs. Then she squatted behind one of the jerseys. When the milk was making a rhythmic sound on the bottoms of the pails, Lucy said, "I've got something to tell you."

Rud, with worry lines about his blue eyes, was lost in a private world—a world that asked how he was going to feed the family and set aside a little money if the crops didn't perk up. Without thinking, he said, "I got something to tell you, too. I been looking at the cotton. It didn't come up good in the first place. That last rain put the river over it. Water's gone down, but the stalks are as yellow as a pumpkin and not more than half a stand. The corn looks good, but the cane is as spindly as the hair on a dog's hind leg. I was countin' on good crops of cotton and sorghum molasses. If it ain't one thing to worry a feller, it's something else."

"That's the way life is most places," Lucy said. Trying to reassure her husband, she said, "We'll make it. We have to, because we have so much to look forward to. As I was saying, I have got something to tell you. . . ."

Rud had finished stripping his cow. When he stood up, Lucy's voice trailed off. There was a look of despondency on his face that made the news seem burdensome. The joy and the anticipation Lucy had experienced, knowing she was pregnant, slipped away. "We will need the wagon to carry the food and the chairs to the decoration," she said.

When Rud started after the team, it occurred to him that Lucy had tried to tell him something. Halfway across the pasture, he stopped and looked back. Lucy had washed the milk buckets and was turning them upside down on the fence post to sterilize in the sun. Rud whistled to his wife and motioned her toward him.

Old Rang heard the whistle and followed her through the gate. She walked straight across the pasture, but the dog circled the fence row, his reddish tail a flag, darting in and out of the brush in search of a rabbit. He gave a yelp and ran off out of sight. Lucy took Rud's hand.

"It just occurred to me that you were trying to tell me something," Rud said. "Have we time to talk now?"

Lucy nodded. "We've got a couple of hours. Let's look at your squirrel family," she said.

Rud put his arm about her shoulders, and they matched steps until they reached the rocky ledge. In the vine-covered enclosure, Lucy stretched her legs on the surface, and Rud squatted behind her. "Look!" He pointed to the ball of leaves. The move from the nest had marked the end of their childhood, and the leaf nest was a mass of teenage squirrel activity. Like Chipper, they had stubby whiskers, skimpy red fur, and a spare crop of hair on their pencil tails. But the squirrels were growing swiftly now, as if some time clock had been set off in their bodies.

"Look!" Rud said again. "The mother is with them." While they watched, the old squirrel guided her children out on a limb, coaxing them along with soft chirping sounds. Rud had named the largest of the three "Boldly," for he was far more daring then his sisters. Boldly stepped bravely along, but "Timid" and "Shy"held back, whimpering the way Chipper did when she was afraid.

The mother led Boldly to the end of a limb where a grapevine dangled toward the ground. She turned around, but the young squirrel did not follow her back along the branch. He investigated the tip of the limb and then went down the vine. His mother began to scold, but Boldly ignored her until he discovered his folly. Rud and Lucy watched him fight the vine in an effort to turn himself around. But his pawing and clawing sent the vine swinging. Boldly slipped to the tip of it and dangled in midair.

"Mother Squirrel is frantic," Rud whispered, watching her race down the limb in a helpless effort to save her child. Squeaking with terror, Boldly gave one more lunge. He lost his hold and plunged downward. "There's the instinct Papa spoke of," Rud said, watching the squirrel's four feet spreading apart. His tail drifted back and forth. Boldly landed on his feet, shaky, but unhurt. As worried as any human mother, the old squirrel raced down the trunk of the tree to examine her child. Finding him unhurt, she slapped his stubborn jaws and charged Boldly up the tree.

Lucy got to her feet when the squirrels disappeared. Without turning to face Rud, she said, "I am going to have a baby in December."

Rud stood there, knowing he loved Lucy more than he had ever loved anyone. But his love was mixed with a kind of anger, born out of fear and desperation. She had forced one child upon him. Now, before he had adjusted to that one with all the extra problems of giving it a normal life, he was to have the added burden of childbirth to worry about. Having lost Ruth, he knew a woman needed more help than Granny was able to give at a time like that. With the nearest doctor fourteen miles away (or a thousand for all practical purposes), should there be heavy rain or snow—it was enough to drive a man crazy just thinking about what could happen. But Rud wasn't one to show cowardice. Bending, he kissed the back of her neck. "What a Christmas present," he said and let it go at that.

They left the ledge, and Rud found his mules down near the river. He led them into the barn for a couple of ears of corn apiece before he harnessed them.

Lucy packed her dinner in two bushel baskets which Papa brought in. Then she hurried into a puff-sleeved dress, which she had made from a piece of lavender voile, bought before she was married. With the voile material, Lucy had purchased three yards of white linen. From that, she had made Corky a new suit. She helped the child into it and was combing his hair when Esther knocked at the door.

"I want to show her my new suit," Corky said. Lucy gave him a little shove, and he strutted across the room with Chipper perched on his shoulder.

Corky opened the door, and Esther, full of complimentary praise, stepped inside with a basket in one hand and a chocolate cake in the other. Chipper recognized her immediately. Esther set her food by the side of the door, and the squirrel leaped into her arms.

"She likes you better than she does Billy Higs," Corky said.

"I know why," Esther said. "That hound follows Billy and sleeps with him, too, I imagine. Chipper's sharp sense of smell and her instinct tell her the dog is to be feared."

"Not instinct," Corky said. "She knows cuz the hound nearly ate her up."

"What's he talking about?" Esther asked Lucy.

"Corky had Chipper in the front yard a couple of days ago. She started around the house to where Rud was sharpening a plow, and she came head-on with Billy's hound."

"He opened his mouth and would have swallowed Chipper," Corky said, "but she ran right down the front of Daddy's shirt."

While they were laughing at Chipper's escape, Papa came in the front door. Dressed in his best blue shirt and pants, he was carrying a foot tub, full of cut roses. Their fragrance followed him toward the kitchen. "I am going to wrap the stems in wet paper," he said.

"It'll make them last longer," Esther said. "I got a bucket of iris out there; wrapped in wet cloths. I won't need all of them to decorate one grave. Thought I'd take some of your roses and you can have part of my iris, if that's alright."

"That's the way we usually work it," Papa called from the kitchen. Then the old man put the food and the flowers in the wagon. Rud loaded the chairs, and the family lumbered their way down the mountain.

The school yard was packed with wagons and stripped-down cars, carrying bouquets, fragrant with morning dew.

Women and girls, in their most colorful best, carried chairs to the red oak shade. Some of the men and boys sat with their womenfolk; others sprawled on the ground. Preacher Adams opened the outdoor service with prayer, asking the Lord to be merciful, to lead sinners to repent, to comfort the afflicted, and to make his children submissive to his will—a will that was mysterious and beyond human understanding. In keeping with the occasion, he said, "We can't understand why a loved one was taken. We can't understand why we have afflictions like pneumonia, typhoid, and all the other diseases that have taken our loved ones." Behind Rud a baby whimpered. And farther back, Beard said, "Amen."

Corky wiggled, and Rud opened his eyes to see what the boy was doing. He was whispering in Lucy's ear; then the woman's hands, red with lye soap and unfamiliar toil, loosened the shirt button at Corky's throat. There was something about Lucy's red hands and the sight of the two graves just beyond them that filled Rud with despair. He could see Mama's red-rough hands, folded on her breast; and above the praying, he could hear Ruth saying, "Help me bring this baby into the world. . . . For God's sake, don't let me die." Rud closed his eyes tight against tears no one but God would ever see. "Lord, help me; help me," Rud whispered.

"Let's sing, 'There Shall Be Showers of Blessing,'" he said. Then everyone began to sing. Rud joined in the singing of hymns that told him: there shall be seasons refreshing; take the name of Jesus with you; lean on the everlasting arms. As he sang, a calmness came over the man. And the preaching that followed made him wonder what troubled folks did when they didn't have the Lord.

The service closed with prayer. Then the congregation began to shake hands, to talk about crops and what the President was doing about hard times, and to ask about old neighbors who had not been seen since they moved away.

Then the women brought their picnic baskets to the long,

rough table, and Rud could smell the pickled beets and the fried chicken. With his mouth watering, he gathered with the rest of the men, along one side of the table. Someone asked the blessing, and then everyone tried to sample a little of everything.

Following the meal, there were several informal talks by visiting ministers and a number of songs by a half dozen quartets. Then the women decorated the graves, while the children played and the men talked.

Rud carried one of the chairs to a shade, which was filled with old-timers. He found a level spot for his chair. When he sat down, Corky, following close behind, tried to get on his lap. Then Rud heard a little girl say, "You want to come and play?"

Rud was pleased to hear Corky say, "I don't care," and the girl led him away.

Above the murmur of male voices, Rud heard the girl say, "You sit right here. We are going to put on a program. First, you'll hear from the Stoker sisters." Rud watched a group of children who were sitting in front of a make-believe stage. Then three little girls, the oldest not more than ten, began to sing and act out a song.

"I am tired of your old program," a boy yelled when the next act came on. After some argument, part of the children made a circle and began to sing, "We're marching 'round the levee." But Corky's friend drew a hopscotch game and suggested Corky and another boy play with her. "But girls always go first," she reminded them. Rud watched her throw a piece of glass into the first square. With one foot tucked back, she hopped up in the air and came down again as gracefully as a sparrow.

In time, she stepped on a line. "It's your turn," she told Corky. He threw his piece of glass, folded up his leg, and landed with the grace of a crippled chicken. Rud felt the urge to help him. Then he heard the girl laughing. "Boys look so funny playing hopscotch," she said. "Why do you put your foot out front instead of curving it back like this?"

"I dunno," a boy with perfect sight said. And Rud watched him hop like a lame goose, his leg out front, and then he fell over sideways. Corky and the little girl rolled with laughter.

Satisfied that Corky was enjoying himself, Rud's ears tuned in the men. Voicing the political views of most of the hillfolk, Af said, "I-doggies, I'm het up with them fellers up in Washington, 'specially them New Dealers that's supposed to know so much about farm problems. When it comes to killin' livestock and controllin' crops, I'm agin it."

"I agree," Beard said. "But Roosevelt is a Democrat, and I keep hoping. . . ."

"Listen, I want to tell you a good'un," Sam Rankin cut in. "It seems this here feller found a joint snake in his backyard. He whacked it with a hoe. And true to nature, the joint snake flew all apart. The thing lay there long enough to convince the feller it was dead, and then the joints began to reassemble. The farmer knew the habits of joint snakes, how they go back together when left alone. So he hid a two-inch section in his pocket. For several minutes the head and the tail searched the ground for the missing link. When it could not be found, the snake coupled in a corncob, stuck out its tongue, and crawled away."

Rud slapped his leg with the rest of the men. Then he said, "It's easy to see you been talking to one of them drummers that pass by the store. The joint snake reminds me of the story about the coachwhip. Now you fellers know how a coachwhip can wrap itself around a guy and flail a person to death."

The circle of faces leaned forward, heads nodded, and everyone grinned. Beard said, "He's a-kiddin', but I—gosh, they'll do it. Sometimes two snakes will gang up with one snake holding a person while the other one does the whipping."

Rud grinned, and his blue eyes were mischievous. "I'm not under oath, friends, so this story may or may not be true. But I have it from the horse's mouth that this here feller was walking down the road when he met a coachwhip. The snake took after him, and the feller ran until he was all out of breath. Having no better solution, he ran to a hickory tree and clung to the trunk, knowing the snake couldn't whip if he couldn't get a hold of him. True to nature, the coachwhip tried to wrap itself around the feller, but it wasn't long enough to reach around the tree. Now a less determined species would have given up. But a coachwhip is a mule-headed sort, and the thing kept trying until it flailed itself to death."

The men roared with laughter and then quieted down, each searching his mind for a better story. Above the chatter and the laughter of the women and the children, a jangle of harnesses could be heard. A bumblebee buzzed, and a mocking bird, sharing the tree with the men, shouted his disapproval.

The isolation of the Ozarks had sharpened man's imagination and produced some excellent storytellers. With no other form of entertainment available, their eyes and ears were alert to the unusual or the ridiculous in anything and everyone, including themselves. The men had learned to glean an incident, to polish, to change, and finally to entertain without hurt to anyone. Most of their stories began; "There was this here feller." Rud found the manner in which a story was told as interesting as the tale itself. It was alright to express mild doubt if you were a veteran member of the story session. But an outsider, if he was trusted enough to be included, must never voice doubt. Mostly the men told their yarns to a proven audience, where the mood and the setting was just right. Since Decoration Day was a time for honoring their dead, eventually their stories focused on the deeds of some departed.

"It's a fine day for decoration," Beard said. Then pointing a bony finger to a flower-covered plot, he added, "There lays one of the best bee-trackers in the country."

Heads nodded in agreement. Then a visiting preacher said, "Speaking of bees reminds me of a fellow I met during my first pastorate over in Madison County. Folks were poor as dirt, and weddings were the only thing I got paid for. That pay came in the form of chickens, eggs, and at one time, beeswax, which brought a fair price. One day this here fellow came to me wanting to get married. 'I got some beeswax,' he said.

"I looked at the wax, and I knew right off it wouldn't buy the makings of one small meal. I was young then, didn't have a crop or anything, and Lord, I was hungry. Trying for something I could eat, I said, 'There's not half enough beeswax here. You will have to bring me a chicken.'

"'I could work for you,' the man said. I told him I didn't have any work I couldn't do myself. The girl, a ragtag little thing, worried a minute and then she said, 'Couldn't you marry us just far enough for it to be legal and then complete the ceremony when we find another bee tree?'"

Amid hoots of laughter, Af said, "I don't know about you, Preacher. Sometimes I think you dream these tales up. Then you tell them so often we get to believing 'em!"

"You mean he's like this here feller I used to know," Sam Rankin began. "Ross, I think his name was. I can't remember. But I know he was a dudish sort that liked to put on the dog. His high-minded notions kept him in a bind, and most of the time he didn't have the money to buy a postage stamp.

"He married right after he came to Newton County, and he was trying to farm when word reached him his pa was dying. Not having the price of a train fare, Ross set off on foot. He had a dollar bill between him and the state of Tennessee. As luck would have it, a logger picked him up and took him all the way to Little Rock. Being a proud man, Ross made up a heartbreaking story about being robbed. He said some fellers took his wagon, a team, and five hundred dollars. His sick pa and the robbery story aroused the truck driver's sympathy. At the end of the line, he found another driver that took Ross all the way to Memphis. In the course of the trip, going there and coming back, Ross told his story so many times he got to believing it. When he got home, he kissed his woman. Then he said, 'Sit down, Bulah. I got bad news. I hadn't gone fifty miles before I was robbed. Some fellers took my wagon, the team, and our five hundred dollars!' "

Papa, the more serious of the group, said, "Wasn't Bulah the woman who killed a panther?"

"That she was," Beard said. "I know that for a fact."

For the benefit of the younger men, Papa continued in his no-nonsense way. "The folks moved here about the time my mother did. They built a two-room cabin, and the windows had no glass in them. Every once in a while Bulah would hear a panther, but she wasn't scary like most women. She'd tote a gun when she carried the baby and the washing down to the spring.

"Well, one day her man went to the county seat, and he didn't get back before dark. When milking time came, Bulah got the baby to sleep and left it in the house. When she came back, there was a panther in the house, and it had the baby in its mouth. The cat was between Bulah and the gun. So she grabbed the best weapon she could find—a double-bit ax her man had left on the front porch. The panther crouched, ready to leap through the window, but Bulah raised the ax, and she laid the panther's head wide open. Funny thing about it, the baby didn't wake up until it hit the floor."

"That Bulah was spunky alright," Af said. "If I remember correctly, her man was a fine bee hunter. Seems they always had plenty of honey."

"I used to be good as you'll find," Beard said. "All a person needs is a can of sweet anise and keen eyesight. I used to soak corncobs in sweet anise and lay them on stumps. In no time a-tall, they would attract wild bees. I was a fast walker in those days and didn't have any trouble trackin' a bee."

"I know a feller that never looks for a tree of his own," someone said. "Fact is, I don't think he's got sense enough to know a bee when he sees it. So what does he do? He cuts the trees other folks find and clearly mark. I maintain that it takes the rottenest puke alive to cut another feller's bee tree."

"I agree, but not altogether," Af said. "As I see it,

Washington has some of the worst pukes alive. Who else would tell folks to plow up part of their crops?"

The hills echoed with similar opinions. But Beard tried to reassure the crowd. "Look at it this way: Roosevelt's a Democrat. Things always get better when a Democrat gets in, don't you say so?"

"Usually," the reluctant crowd finally agreed. "Sure it does," the old man soothed. "And I'm a-hopin' things will get better in Washington any day now."

Rud watched Lucy gathering up the bits of food left on her platters. Wondering where his next sack of flour was coming from, he was a-hoping, too. But Rud was hoping things would get better a little closer to home.

Chapter Seven

A TIME OF TROUBLE

As the summer wore on, Rud's cotton crop became increasingly hopeless. It was obvious he would have to get work away from the farm if he was to save any money whatsoever.

To keep from going in debt at the store, Rud traded a shoat to Sam, a fair-dealing man, who owned not only the store, but also the grist mill and a sorghum mill that he operated in season. With a rope on the hog's leg, Rud took it down to the merchant's pen.

"I'll do the best I can for you," Sam said, when the fly-specked screen slammed behind Rud.

Leaning on a distorted glass counter, where penny candy was sold, Rud inhaled the mixed fragrance of feed, fruit, dust, and dry goods. "I know that, Sam. You're not a guy to cheat a feller."

He watched the heavyset, already balding young man plunk down fifty pounds of flour and a five-pound bag of salt. Then he weighed up three pounds of coffee and ten pounds of sugar, enough staples to keep stomach and soul together until the crops were laid by.

Meanwhile, Rud plowed and Lucy hoed in spite of his objections, because Papa was down with fever and chills. Rud spent his last dime on quinine. When Papa got better, Rud hid his gnawing fears behind a frail plan. As soon as the last row was laid by, he was going to work at the sawmill, back in the hills where Frank and Billy were working. It would mean being away from home for a week or more at a time, but with his team, he would earn a dollar a day. That, along with whatever cotton he made, and the dozen buckets of sorghum he would have to sell, Rud figured he could save a little toward a doctor for Lucy and the boy's operation.

Rud finished his plowing the last part of July. When he came in from the field, he put his mules in a stall. Frank and Billy were coming by about four the next morning. Rud wanted the animals corralled. He put some corn nubbins in the mules' trough. Above their crunching, he heard Lucy throwing hay to the cows. Feeling suddenly prankish, he slipped around the side of the barn, intending to surprise his wife from behind. Lucy was standing at a side door. As Rud approached, she turned and pitched a forkful of hay into his face. "Watch it!" Rud yelled and gave his wife a playful shove. Lucy, unmindful of her condition, took up the tomboy game, and the two of them fell over in the hay, laughing like a couple of children. When they quieted down, Rud said, "The crops are in shape. I'm headin' for the sawmill in the morning. That means I won't be seeing you for a couple of weeks."

"I know it's necessary. But I hate to see you go," Lucy said. She sat up, and Rud helped her pick the straw from her hair. When the milking was done, they walked to the house, arm-in-arm, their spare hands swinging two buckets of milk.

Rud lay awake for a long time that night thinking about their short marriage. He had learned in those months that there were no disappointments Lucy could not take, no drudgery she was afraid to tackle. His wife rubbed the clothes, worked the garden, hoed the fields, canned vegetables, and took care of her chickens like a veteran.

On Sunday she played the church piano, taught Sunday School in a teacher's absence, and as was her nature, helped take care of sick children in the neighborhood. In the path of moonlight that poured across their bed, Rud looked at his wife. Her dark hair framed a face that was childlike in sleep. Wishing he could make life just a little easier for her, Rud fell asleep.

Rud's days in the woods were more or less alike—days filled with back-breaking work behind a mule and a log, with the good-natured kidding of other loggers, the buzzing of the saw, and the smell of fresh sawdust. At night Rud ate his share of beans and corn bread and then watched the stars twinkling through the cracks in the three-sided shelter around his bed.

The first week out the crew worked until Saturday evening; then those close enough to go home did so. Rud, Frank, and Billy were eight rough miles from home, and they decided to stay around the camp.

As darkness fell, and the drum of katydids jarred through the trees, Frank in his smelly overalls lit a lantern, took out his knife, and began to whittle. Rud opened a western magazine one of the men had left and was flipping the pages when a dog barked down by the river. Frank's head shot up, and his hands froze on the piece of pine. "Is that Trumpet?" he asked.

The Higs' hound heard his name and stirred. Then the thump, thump, thump of his leg was heard against the board under Rud's feet. Grinning, Rud said, "Why don't you do something about them fleas? They're eatin' that hound alive."

Frank pushed his sweat-stained straw hat to the back of his head, resumed his whittling, and with his eyes on the wood, said, "Fleas are a hound's salvation. All that twisting and clawing keeps his joints from gettin' stiff. That's why he can outrun any fox in the county."

Billy, quietly curled on his bunk, said, "It'd be a good night for a chase. Moon's full. I hate to be inside on a moonlit night. Much ruther be out chasing a coon."

Frank tapped his knife thoughtfully against his boot heel and listened. After a minute, he shook his head. "I don't care much for light nights. Varmints get shy, don't move around much. Still that is a mighty sweet sound. Like as not it's an old fox. Bet he's hemmed up in one of them caves down by the river."

Billy bounced out of the shack. His dark eyes had a wild, determined gleam. "You two can stay if you want to. I'm a-goin'."

Frank shot to his feet. Rud, in no mood to stay alone, dropped his magazine. Trumpet, getting the message, forgot his tormentors. Cocking one red ear toward the river, he gave one throaty sound and trotted off, his nose making snuffling sounds over every leaf and stick as he followed an invisible path toward the river.

The dog followed a steep course toward the river. Though there was no visible path, undergrowth was short in the heavy timber, and the moonlight, outlining the dark shadows, was a silvery white. When the river could be seen below them, Trumpet got a whiff of something. He raised his head for a quavering, exultant "Yoooooo," then he took off, adding his yelps to that of the other dog.

To Rud's experienced ear, the baying told a story. At first Trumpet's voice was hesitant and indecisive beside the other dog. Then he became certain, and the voices became a steady rhythm that was music to the ears of most of the mountain men.

When the men reached the river, they fought their way through a viny thicket and came out in a clearing a few feet from the dogs. "That's funny," Frank said. "They got something backed up to a tree."

Billy rushed forward, but then took a few steps back. "You dang right! He's backed up to a tree, and that ain't no fox. That's a wildcat!"

Rud stepped closer. Behind the lunging hounds a wildcat, with ears laid back, was hissing and snarling, daring the dogs to close in.

"Lord-a-mercy, we need a gun," Billy said. Then the cat broke between the dogs and made a dash into the thicket, looking ruffled and ill-tempered. The dogs took after him, but Rud called them off. "What you do that for?" Billy asked.

Ignoring Billy's question, Rud patted Trumpet's head. "Come on you flea-bitten bag of bones. You've given us enough excitement for tonight," he said, leading the dogs back up the mountain.

When the second Friday came, Rud started home. With eleven dollars in his pocket, he took off on one of his mules, leaving the other mule with Frank and Billy, who were at home in the woods.

Rud rode through the sunset and the twilight hours. Above the clopping of the animal's hoofs, Rud's ears caught the whisper of the trees, the sounds of insects, and the chirping of roosting birds. As he neared Pleasant Ridge, long after dark, the moon climbed the mountain with him. When the harness jangled up the last incline, he saw Lucy listening for him on the front porch. She had heard the sound of the mule and was waiting at the front gate when Rud got there.

He swung off the mule and put his arms about his wife, expecting a kiss. When it did not come, Rud said, "What's this? No loving for the weary?" He raised her chin, and he saw her eyes were red from crying. Rud's eyes searched the porch for Papa. "What's happened?" he asked, expecting something to be wrong with the old man.

"Papa's fine," Lucy's voice quavered. "It's Corky. He's down, complaining of headache, backache, and he's having stomach pains, something terrible."

Rud struggled against a rising fear—his voice was flat as he said, "Anything else?"

"Yes," Lucy went on. "There is a rash. At first I thought it was measles, but I know better now."

In the same flat voice Rud said, "It sounds like typhoid.

Didn't Papa tell you? He ought to have known. Mama had the same symptoms."

In the moonlight Rud could see Lucy's face, a composed face now that he was there. If she was afraid or worried, it did not show. Her pale face showed determination that the two of them could lick any problem. Rud did not feel all that brave. Fear was drying his mouth and tightening his muscles. A man is so darn helpless up against something like this, he told himself. He's supposed to be strong, to have solutions. He ran his tongue over his sun-parched lips. "It may not be typhoid," he spoke, reassuring himself as much as his wife. "I'll take out the mules. Then I'll crank up the truck. The important thing is to get a doctor."

He yanked off the harness, and the chains clanked against the spike nail that held them on the side of the barn. Again he heard that tiny quaver in Lucy's voice. "It's typhoid alright. Granny Sellers is here. Papa's gone after the doctor."

"But why?" Rud asked, weak with the memory of two summers ago.

"It has to be the well," Lucy said. "I had Papa nail it up. We will carry water from the spring until it is tested."

Numb with the news, Rud followed Lucy's heavy figure into the house and up the stairs. Granny was sitting beside the child; she had a pan of water in one hand, a washrag in the other. On the bed, Corky tossed and muttered in a senseless, disconnected way. Already the air in the room was foul with the smell of sickness. Rud pulled up a chair and sat down beside the old woman. Gently he began a one-way conversation about the squirrels and how Chipper was waiting for him to get well. Corky opened his eyes and stared at the man, but they were wild and unseeing with fever.

Rud picked up a spoon that was lying beside a glass on the night stand. With the handle, he forced Corky's mouth open and looked at the boy's tongue. It was coated a dirty brown. He pulled up his nightshirt and touched the swollen stomach. Corky let out a scream of pain. "How long has he been like this?" Rud asked.

"Five days. As I said, I thought it was measles," Lucy began.

"Is the water fresh from the spring?" Rud cut in.

"It's fresh. I brought it up just before dark," Granny answered him.

"Then we've got to keep sponging him," Rud said. "We've got to keep the fever down."

"I've been doin' just that," Granny said kindly. "But here, you take the pan and the washrag, and I'll keep the water nice and cold."

Rud sponged the child for more than an hour. Papa returned then with Dr. Shedd. The old doctor examined the child as Rud had done. Then he measured out a spoon of white powder, mixed it with a little water, and forced it down Corky's throat. The man set a blue medicine bottle on the stand. "Give him that according to directions," he said. "Keep up the sponging. Try to get his fever down. I'll be back in a couple of days. Not much else I can do though."

Rud did not leave the child's bed that night. But he fell asleep when Corky quieted down at daybreak. Half an hour later, the sun, touching his face, awakened Rud. He grunted, got up from the chair, and tried to stretch some of the stiffness from his muscles. Granny had left him and was downstairs making coffee. When she returned, Granny said, "There's a health man downstairs. Lucy wants you to come down and talk to him about the well."

Lucy and Papa had their backs to the stairs. The stranger facing them nodded when Rud came down. "My name is Rogers," he said. "I have tested your water, Mr. Marshall. It's contaminated. I'd say you are getting some seepage from the barn lot. Better use your spring until you can dig another well. I tested the spring. It's pure."

Rud thanked the man, and the screen door slammed between them. "It's going to be a heck of a job hauling water up that hill," Papa muttered. "But there's nothing we can do about it. Seems if it ain't one thing, it's another. Still, I reckon we got a lot to be thankful for. And I ain't going to complain about nothing if our kid will just get well." Papa's faded eyes filled with tears. He said something about having to feed the hogs and hurried out of the house.

For the next five days, Rud did not stretch out in a bed, and Lucy did so reluctantly. Sometimes Rud would awake in his chair and find Lucy sponging the child. Then Granny would come fussing into the room and insist that Lucy get some sleep for the baby's sake. The lamp did not go out during those nights. Neighbors came in shifts, bringing food and encouragement. Ignoring the possibility of contagion, Af and Beard helped sponge their young friend, and along with other neighbors sat out the long nights with the Marshalls.

From experience, Rud and most of the other folk knew the dreaded signs of approaching death. There were times when Corky had all of them. The child was exhausted, he vomited blood, and the pains in his stomach increased until they had to hold him down on the bed. Then one morning there was such a rapid fall in temperature, Rud asked Granny to take Lucy outside, certain the end was near. The old woman put a dip of snuff in her lip and put her thumb on Corky's wrist. When she looked up, her eyes had a new twinkle. "He's got a strong pulse. Fever broke awful quick, but I'd say he's goin' to be alright."

Later that day, Lucy boiled a chicken down low and skimmed all the fat from the broth. Every half hour Granny fed Corky the broth, beginning with a teaspoonful and increasing it until the child could take a fourth of a cup at a time. A couple of days later Corky was craving store-bought bread—"light bread." Since Rankin's store did not carry such perishables, Rud cranked up the truck and made the fourteen-mile trip to Jasper. With the pocket change left from paying for the doctor and the medicine, Rud bought Corky two loaves.

Now that Corky was feeling better, Chipper was allowed in his room. Propped against his pillows, Corky watched her acting like a cross between a playful puppy and a frolicsome kitten. He made a twine ball, and when he tossed it, Chipper brought the ball back to him. Sometimes he would drag a piece of red yarn along the covers, and the little squirrel would run after it. Once in a while, a fiber of the yarn caught on her tongue. Then she would spit and wipe her mouth while Corky laughed.

Squirrel fashion, she was up at the crack of dawn. First she went down to the box of hickory nuts Corky kept for her in the corner of the kitchen. After some loud gnawing and a shower of hulls, she went to her water pan, drank, and groomed herself. Then instinct told her to plant some nuts for the future. Grabbing one in her mouth, the squirrel scurried up the stairs to Corky's room, dug in his cover, planted the nut, and patted it down.

Every now and then she took a notion to plant the nuts in Rud and Lucy's bed. When that happened, Rud threw a shoe at her, chasing the squirrel back to Corky's room.

When Corky was well enough to be outside, Rud carried him to their rock ledge, overlooking the squirrel tree. It was a Saturday morning, and there was a hint of rain in the air. From the vine enclosure, Rud saw the mother squirrel scurrying around on the pebbled beach below. She found an acorn, sat back on her haunches, and cut away the hull. When the tidbit was gone, she washed her face in nervous laps and swats, pausing every few seconds to look about. She completed her facial and started to clean her body. Then Rud heard a squeak, and in the next flash the squirrel darted up the tree. "Something must have scared her," Rud whispered, looking around. Across the river he saw old Trumpet moving like a shadow toward the stream. "I guess Frank and Billy are home for the weekend," Rud said.

The hound crossed the river, his tail curved over his backbone and his nose on the ground. He snuffled the stones around the tree. The mother squirrel ran out on a limb, and from her safe perch, she fluffed her tail. "Chad! Chad! Chad!" she scolded in a high, excited voice.

"I think she's telling that hound to get," Corky said. Rud

agreed. But the dog paid no attention, and the squirrel's vocal expression rose until she was chirring like a small motor. All the while her tail was lashing from side to side or standing straight up with the tip twitching. "I see the young ones in the leaf house," Rud said. "Or I should say, I see the tips of their noses."

Finally the dog trotted on his way, and the squirrel calmed down. Tired from her emotional outburst, she flattened herself on a branch, looking like a larger Chipper, asleep on the foot of Corky's bed.

While they watched, a cloud had moved in from the west, and the sound of thunder brought Rud to his feet.

"If we don't hurry, we are going to get wet," he said, stooping to pick up Corky. As he did so, a sad cooing directed Rud's eyes to a limb a little lower than the ledge. When the first drops of rain touched his cheek, Rud looked into one of the flimsiest nests he had ever seen. Describing it to Corky, Rud said, "If there weren't four eggs in that pile of sticks and a dove nearby, I would never take it for a nest at all."

"I wish I could see it," Corky said wistfully. Then he added for the first time, "When I get my operation, I'll see everything, won't I, Daddy?" The yearning in the child's voice was a stab in Rud's heart. "That you will," he said, his long legs moving swiftly through the rain.

Soaked to the skin, Rud opened the back door. The smell of freshly baked cookies greeted their noses, and Lucy with flour on her hands began to fuss about Corky being wet. Over a sheet of dough, she said, "You want him to take a backset? Take him upstairs. Dry him off good and get him into dry clothes."

"I feel good," Corky assured his mother. At the sound of his voice, Chipper came out of hiding and ran up his back to perch on the boy's shoulder. Puzzled at his wet shirt, she squeaked unhappily and hopped over to the top of the kitchen safe.

"Honestly," Lucy shook her head. "I don't know what we are going to do with that little varmint," she said. "Her toenails are wearing out the curtains, and she has gnawed the broom handle down half its size."

"What makes squirrels gnaw?" Corky asked Rud.

"Let's get out of these wet clothes. Then I'll tell you," Rud said.

When the men came back to the kitchen, the table was set for noon-time dinner. The plates were turned neatly over the bone-handled knives and forks. The spoon jar stood in the middle of the table, and the toothpick vase stood beside it. The menfolk sampled a cookie while Lucy dished up fresh garden vegetables.

Not one to forget a question, Corky said, "You were going to tell me what makes a squirrel gnaw."

Rud removed Chipper from her perch on the safe. He forced the kicking, clawing animal's mouth open so Corky could see her teeth. "She is a member of the rodent family, which means 'gnawing animal,'" Rud said. "A rodent's teeth grow all the time. The enamel on the back is softer than it is on the front. This gives her teeth a razor-sharp edge. That's why she had no trouble cutting through a hickory nut hull."

"That is also why she enjoys the broom handle," Lucy put in.

While they were waiting for the corn bread to brown, Rud took out his pocketknife. "I am going to trim her toe nails," he said. "That will keep her from running up and down the window curtains. But there isn't much we can do about her gnawing habits."

When Lucy removed her pan of bread from the oven, Rud washed his hands and Corky called Papa to dinner. Around the table Corky told the old man about the strange nest Rud had seen in the squirrel tree.

"What kind of nest would that be?" Lucy asked.

Papa poured his coffee into a saucer to cool and said: "That's a turtledove nest. I'll tell you something that's as strange as that pile of sticks they nest on. Unlike other birds, doves do not feed their young bugs and worms. They feed the little birds something called 'pigeon milk.' That means the male and female digest food in their stomachs. Then they spit it up and feed it to the young. As a boy, I was told I would make a trip in the direction of the first turtledove I heard cooing," Papa said. Then he added, "There is a beautiful Bible verse that speaks of the turtledove. Remind me and we'll use it for our family reading tonight."

The rain and the thunder continued throughout the afternoon and the evening. But it began to break away about bedtime. In the quietness of the passing storm, Corky reminded Papa of the Bible passage. The old man put on his wire-rimmed glasses, opened the well-worn book, and began to read:

> For, lo, the winter is past, the rain is over and gone; The flowers appear on the earth; the time of the singing of birds is come, and the voice of the turtle is heard in our land (Song of Solomon 2:11-12, KJV).

Chapter Eight

HELPING HANDS

Sunday afternoon Rud went back to his sawmill job. Coming home Friday nights to make certain the family was alright, he worked through August and the first week of September. Then Rud started home to stay, for the cane was ready to make molasses, and whatever cotton he would have to pick would soon be opening.

The August days behind Rud were the hottest for the summer. When he started home, riding one mule and leading the other, he was grateful for the little breeze that rose when the sun set. There had been no rain since Rud left home, and the grasshoppers made a "tick, tick" sound in the brittle grass on either side of the trail. As the shadows grew, wildlife, which had been stilled by the heat, began to move about. At a creek crossing, a flock of crows scattered, cawing as they went. Rud paused to let the mules drink. Above the sipping and the trinkle of the little stream, Rud could hear the raven sentinel cawing from the top of a dead tree.

Ignoring the ruckus, a chipmunk flung the dirt from her burrow and scurried down to the water's edge to drink with the mules.

As the animals raised their long heads and spit at the bits, Rud urged them on. Clopping down the mountain path, the mules showed weariness in their heavy, deliberate movements. Rud was glad the hard work was over for them. Bess, the gentler of the two, would have to turn the molasses mill. Then the mules would be free until next spring. Rud gave the animal's brown, gray-flecked neck an appreciative pat and then sat back. His long legs dangled with the jangling harness, and there was an aura of fatigue about the blue eyes which stared from the man's Indian-tanned face.

For miles in a houseless stretch of forest, Rud was aware of one sound only, the clopping of hoofs inching him homeward. Then the misty gray of twilight caught up with him, and the soft murmur of crickets swelled in their nightly chorus. When night came, it was black, for the moon, looking like a sliver of cantaloupe, gave very little light. Whippoorwills began their frenzied song; the mournful hoot of an owl came from the hollow below. Finally Rud passed a leaning structure with the sounds and scents of livestock. A mile farther, he saw four squares of light. The lamp light and the voices he heard beyond meant home to him—but it meant something else, also, and Rud felt his muscles tense. There was too much light, too many voices, and he could see the outline of vehicles in the yard.

He urged the mule forward. Then Papa met him, ready to relieve him of the animals and to explain the wagons, the jalopies, and the horse tied to the fence post. "Some of the neighbors been helping me dig a well," he said. "Beard was telling me about this pickin', fiddlin' group that's visiting with his sister. He thought it would be kind of nice to ask them to play for the folks—you know, as a sort of favor for the work they've done on the well. I hope you ain't too tired to enjoy it."

"No, no," Rud said, trying to straighten his back. "I don't

get too tired to listen to good picking."

"Another thing I better mention," Papa paused, seeming uncertain. "Some of the young folks asked Lucy about square dancing, and she thought it would be alright. I wasn't for it. But seeing they ain't got much else to do, I don't guess there'll be much harm in it."

"I see what you mean," Rud said. But he wasn't prepared for the sight that met his eyes. When he opened the screen door, he found the furniture moved back. The floor, mopped with sandstone, was slick enough to skate on.

Lucy ran to meet him, her face flushed with pleasure and her eyes bright. "The young folks are having such a good time, and the old ones too, if I'm any judge," she said, leading Rud to Beard, who introduced him to the band.

"This is Bill," Beard said. A red-faced guitar player held out his hand.

"This feller can pick anything," a teenaged fiddler said, "anything from a guitar to a chicken!" Beard started to introduce some more of the men, but the band had warmed up and was ready to go.

A young man stepped to the middle of the room. "Choose your squares," he called. The young folks ran about the room until four squares were ready on the big floor. The girls twisted their fingers in front of them. The boys tapped their feet, self-conscious and eager for the music to start. Around the wall the old folks sat, mothers nursing babies, grandmothers holding older children, old men grinning, their minds recalling the best fiddle player they had ever run across.

The caller held up his hand. "All ready?" The squares nodded. "Then let her roll!"

Rud found an empty chair by the doorway that led to the kitchen. Eyeing the table, covered with an assortment of cakes, he sat down as the musicians led off on "Down Yonder." Shrill and clear the fiddles skirled; a harmonica, nasal and sharp, backed them up, and a guitar boomed on the bass strings at the right intervals.

As the caller named the turns, the squares moved, dancing back and forth. "Hands around, swing your partner," he called. The young man tapped his feet, strutted back and forth, going through the figures as he called them. "Swing your partner and do-si-do. Now all join hands and away we go." The music rose and fell. The band broke into "Soldier's Joy," and the feet of young and old around the room kept time with the tune. "Swing to left, now swing to the right. Break now, break now, back to back." Perspiration beaded the young men's brows, and the girls' marcelled hair fell damply about their faces. A half hour later, the music stopped.

When the dancers moved off the floor, laughing and panting, the children rushed on, sliding and shoving. Rud saw Corky slip up behind a boy, pull his hair, and run. The boy turned, caught him, and they fell to the floor. They wrestled around boy-fashion, got up, and ran some more. It was obvious to Rud, all were having a good time, from the oldest to the youngest.

The band members stood up and stretched themselves. Then Beard requested a special number, and the guitarist cut loose on "Charley's neat and Charley's sweet; Charley he's a dandy."

In the background Rud heard a little girl saying, "Pull a hair between your fingers. If it curls, your sweetheart loves you. If it stays straight, that means he has forgotten you."

"I don't believe you," another child said. "But I'll try it just for fun."

"Choose your partner for a waltz," the caller said. The guitar player experimented with the strings, while young men with long hair dangling over their eyes, sauntered about, looking for a partner. Several couples walked onto the floor, and the harmonica player led out on "Red River Valley."

Then the caller asked for special requests. "I got one," Af said. "I'd like to hear Granny Sellers sing 'Barbry Allen,' while you folks play."

Granny had done a lot of ballad singing in her younger days. Her voice, though scratchy with age, was still well suited to that kind of song. Pleased to be asked, she took her place in front of the band. "I have heard this song was written for someone called Hugh of Lincoln, away back in 1255," she said. "I don't know nothing about him, except he must 'a' been a trifling man." The guitar player gave the old woman a note, and she began to sing.

Granny finished her song, and everyone cheered. When she sat down, the young man that had called the numbers stood before the group. "It's obvious we've been a big surprise to someone here tonight," he began. "And we're a-hoping he'll be more surprised as the night progresses."

Rud, still sitting by the doorway, looked about him. More people had arrived, until he would have guessed something like seventy people were spilling out of the house onto the porch. Wondering who was going to be surprised, he heard the caller say, "Our host has a little boy. As most of you know, the child needs an operation. When Beard told me about Rud Marshall, I couldn't believe all the troubles the man has had. I mentioned him to the fellows here, and they wanted to play a little benefit. From where I stand, it looks like everyone is having a whale of a time." A burst of applause filled the room. The caller grinned. Then he said, "We've got a dozen cakes in there to sample. Before the women starts dishin' that treat up, I'm going to ask Beard to pass his hat. Anything you can give will help that frolicking towhead to see—like them boys he's chasing across the room."

Grinning through his whiskers, Beard passed his hat among the menfolk. Rud saw his neighbors and people he did not even know reach into their pockets. Too stunned to speak, he heard the clang of silver—money he knew the people needed themselves.

Lucy left the cake she was slicing and pushed her way to her husband. When Beard hobbled back with the hat, he said, "There's eighteen dollars and some few cents. It's not much, but the old folks don't have much. And the young—they ain't got nothing."

Overwhelmed, Rud stood up. "Some kind of thanks is in order," he said. "But I'm no good at words—specially not at a time like this—" he faltered, searching for words.

Coming to his rescue, the caller said, "A speech is one thing we don't want. We would rather have cake. So, women, lets get on with the servin'."

While the women were serving cake and sending the kids to the porch so they wouldn't get crumbs on the floor, Rud met the man that had initiated the get-together.

"This is Hank Willis," Beard said. Holding out his hand, Rud looked down at a small, graceful man. His blue eyes were too big and too long lashed to belong to a man. But his jaws were dark in spite of a close shave, and his full mouth smiled readily. "Hank and this gang of his has been on the 'Grand Ole Opry,' a few times," Beard went on. "He's my sister's nephew by marriage. They're from down around Nashville."

Fatigue and the surprise of the evening had Rud in a state of shock. "I'm much obliged for all you've done," he said. Then he asked, "What are you folks doing around here?"

"We've been playing for tourists over at Eureka. I grew up around there. I like to come home every now and then. This summer I've gotten reacquainted with some of the old songs such as Granny sang tonight. I've written some of them down. I thought it would be interesting to compare them with the Tennessee version of the same songs. Did you know some of them songs are four or five hundred years old?"

"I knew some of them were old, but I had no idea they were that old," Rud said. Then one of the women put a saucer of cake in the caller's hands and insisted that he come sit down where he would be "nice and comfortable."

When he left Rud, Beard said, "That feller has his share of troubles, too."

"What do you mean?" Rud asked, steering his old friend toward a couple of vacant chairs.

"First of all, he had a boy born to him and his wife that wasn't bright. It tore his wife up so bad she went off her rocker. Woman had to be put in a state hospital. Hank's ma looks after the boy while he's off pickin' and a-callin'. I hear the lad don't know his daddy or anybody else. But Hank's crazy about the kid. He sends most of what he makes home. And he comes back to Eureka every summer to be close to the boy."

Stunned, Rud said, "I thought he was just a kid himself."

"He looks like one, but he's thirty-five or close to it."

Rud looked at the man again. With his new insight, he saw tiny lines about the handsome eyes. But if you weren't looking for them, they were lost in his smile.

"He's a man with a big heart," Rud said. "A man I want Corky to remember."

Later, when everyone was saying goodbye and what a fine time they had, Rud spoke to Sam Rankin about reserving the sorghum mill. "I figure I'll be ready to make my molasses Tuesday. We'll strip the cane tomorrow. Monday, we'll cut it and get it loaded."

Sam checked a notebook he carried in his shirt pocket. "Tuesday is clear." With a stubby pencil poised over the book, he asked, "What time on Tuesday morning you figure on being there?"

"Early. Four—five, at the latest."

Sam was the last of the company to leave. When the door slammed behind him, Rud went straight to bed. Lucy cleaned off the table and followed him, but Rud was so weary he did not know when she got into bed. When he awoke the following morning, the sun was higher than he had intended it to be.

Papa and Corky had already eaten breakfast when Rud came downstairs. "Why didn't you wake me?" he asked.

"I figured you needed the rest," Papa said. "You were all tuckered out last night. I could tell that, just lookin' at you." The old man had two slender boards in his hands, boards they would use to knock the fodder off the cane. "I'm going on to the field," he said. "Take your time. No need to be in too big a hurry."

Papa went outside, and Rud sat down at the table. He opened two biscuits and poured white gravy on top of them. Corky, with Chipper in his arms, sat down next to his dad.

"Your mama milking?" Rud asked.

Corky nodded his head. Then he said, "I was wondering if we could go swimming when you get through in the cane."

Already sweaty in the morning heat, Rud gulped a bite and with another poised on his fork, said, "I can't think of anything else I'd rather do. I got a feeling, I'll be hotter than a biled owl when I come out of that cane patch."

"Mama's been takin' me. And I been takin' Chipper," Corky said. "I know how to swim pretty good now. Chipper's doing pretty good, too."

Over the rim of his coffee cup, Rud looked at the restless, almost-grown squirrel, bucking to free herself from Corky's hands. The slick body slipped through the boy's fingers. She leaped to the floor, and he took off after her, yelling, "Come back here. I can't see you. But I know where you're headin'. You're headin' for my pencil box. You cut up one more pencil, and I won't take you swimming. Remember, I'm a-warning you."

Smiling at Corky's threats, Rud drained his cup, reached for his hat, and went outside.

In a morning sunshine that was already ninety degrees, Rud joined Papa in the field.

"The cane is just right. I like to see a little yellow shine on the stalks. See what I mean?" Papa held a sweet joint for Rud's inspection.

The man nodded. Then he picked up his stripping board and hacked his way down two rows of stalks that towered above his head, blocking what little breeze was stirring.

Papa peeled the cane joint and chewed some of it for sweetness. Then he set to work on the next two rows, keeping pace with his son.

Above the hack, hack of the boards, the curling under-blades crackled under the feet of the men. By midmorning their shirts were plastered wetly to their backs. Their hands were stinging with little blade cuts.

The temperature rose with the sun, but the men worked past the noon hour and finished the stripping before they went to the house for lunch.

Saturday afternoon they cut the cane heads. Leaving the bare stalks to cut and load on Monday, they loaded the seeds and hauled the winter feed to the barn.

The sun had dropped behind the hill when the chores were finished and supper was out of the way. Almost as tired as he had been the night before, Rud changed into an old pair of overalls he used for swimming. Corky, dressed in the same kind of attire, found Chipper, and they started to the river.

The stream was low now, in some places barely running. But the deep pool, clear as drinking water, was an excellent swimming hole, and Rud dove into it.

While he was cooling off, Corky waded, waist-deep, holding his pet. When Rud stood up, his hair pouring over his face, he said, "I thought you could swim."

"I can," Corky assured him. "Stand there and I'll show you." He lowered Chipper into the water, fell forward, and splashed his way to Rud.

The squirrel made a circle and then swam to the shore. In their water play, Rud and Corky forgot Chipper until she screamed "Qua! Qua! Qua!" It was a sound of distress, and they tripped over each other trying to get to her. But before they reached the shore, Rud put his hand on Corky's shoulder. "She's alright," he whispered. "She sees Boldly. He's eating berries that fell from that leaning hackberry tree."

Rud watched Chipper as she ran up the tree, then turned, and chirred at the intruder.

The fat, young male paid her no mind. He scurried around, picking up berries until his appetite was satisfied. Then he took notice of the fussing female, and he started up the tree trunk. The animals made their way toward each other, Boldly sniffing and Chipper quivering. When they were a few inches apart, Chipper screamed and tore into Boldly with a fury Rud had never witnessed in her before.

The squirrels rolled to the ground, bodies locked, their teeth snapping. Hearing the commotion, Corky began to scream, "He'll kill Chipper—I know he'll kill her."

The scream frightened Boldly, and he darted across the ground and up the home tree. A ball of fur floated off in the breeze, and a frazzled-looking Chipper dashed up the hackberry. Rud called her, but she kept going until she reached the top branches. Then she stretched out and wouldn't come down.

At first Rud and Corky were not concerned about the pet. They went back to their swimming, thinking she would come down to join them. But twilight came, the whip-poorwills began to call, and she still had not moved. In the semidarkness, Rud climbed up as far as he dared go in the tree. He reached out and touched the squirrel's tail, but she seemed angry at him, and she crept forward, just out of his reach. The man called and he coaxed until it was so dark he could hardly make his way down out of the horny branches.

"What are we going to do now?" Corky asked when Rud made it back to the ground. The man shook his head, knowing Corky would rather die than leave the pet.

"I guess we'll sit down and wait awhile," he said.

Rud sat down on the tree trunk, letting his feet dangle in the water. Corky sat down beside him. While they waited, the cows came down to the river and drank. The crickets began their nightly song, and a screech owl shrieked on the hill above them. Rud felt a shiver run up Corky's body, and the child moved closer to his dad. "I hate coyotes," he said. "Sometimes I hear 'em at night. I know they can't get in the house. But I hate to hear 'em," he said.

Rud put a protective arm about the child. "There aren't many coyotes in this county," he said. "What you've been hearing is a plain old hound dog. But even if there were coyotes around, you wouldn't need to fear them. Did you know that a coyote family shows affection for one another a lot like us humans?"

Corky shook his head. "They are wolves," he said. "And wolves will eat you up. You want to know how I know?"

"Sure," Rud said, "Tell me."

"Mr. Mann told me about them."

"Who is Mr. Mann?" Rud asked.

"He's the man that lived in that first house—the house we didn't live in when we was by the cotton patch."

"Oh," Rud said. "What else did Mr. Mann tell you?"

"Nothing else. Just that three pigs got ate up by a wolf."

Laughing, Rud said, "I can't argue that story. It's too well known. But I'll tell you what I know about coyotes. When the family members begin to yap, it's kind of like a human songfest. Their songs express high spirits and the joy of being together. When the young boys get together, it's to sing love songs. Their songs aren't at all like the family yapping. Their singing is filled with deep, sad notes, and sometimes, with laughter. The boys sing to attract a mate, and once the lady coyote takes a husband, they stay together. The young couple will dig a tunnel near her parents. When the babies are born, the father lives in a tunnel off from the mother, and listen to this: As soon as the babies are old enough to dig, they dig their own little rooms. In a coyote home, one is likely to find children, parents, and grandparents," Rud said, shifting his weight.

Corky found Rud's last statement amazing. "You mean a coyote family is like our family—with a grandpa and everything?"

"Somewhat," Rud said. "Main thing I'm gettin' at is you don't have to fear animals. They've got a lot of interesting ways if a person will take the time to study them."

"I guess I don't hate 'em like I did," Corky said. Then all was quiet except for a single whippoorwill, the chatter of crickets, and the trinkle of water around their feet. Rud blinked in the darkness, which was broken only by fireflies, and he saw the movement of something at the base of the tree.

Leaning forward, Rud, with his knowledge of animals native to that area, recognized the silvery outline of the moving object as that of an opossum.

The varmint seemed in no hurry, but its destination was obvious when it reached the base of the hackberry tree. Not wanting to share a tree with an opossum, Rud said, "Get away from here."

When he spoke, the wind stirred the leaves ever so lightly, but Chipper must have caught the scent of the stranger. Rud heard her moving down the tree, and in a few seconds she bolted across his lap into Corky's arms.

Rud helped Corky off the tree and up the incline. Halfway across the pasture, they met Papa, coming to look for them. "What in tarnation have you two been up to?" he asked.

Laughing, Rud said, "I am half ashamed to tell you." But Corky saw nothing unusual about sitting in a tree half the night. He was happy to fill his grandpa in on all the details, including the fact that coyotes lived with a grandpa just like he did.

Chapter Nine

MAKING MOLASSES

In a valley shaped by towering mountains, Rankin's crackerbox store leaned toward the matchbox post office, and a two-story gristmill of the same weatherbeaten gray looked like the ghost of a skyscraper. The open sorghum mill, hidden by a pile of cane pulp, was set back against a zigzag fence, overgrown with honeysuckle.

Though dawn was yet to break when Rud and Papa arrived, a flock of hens newly flown from the roost was scratching and clucking in the undergrowth. A white rooster, the leader of the flock, flapped his wings and crowed, and one window in the Rankin house turned yellow with light.

Rud climbed down from the wagon, and Sam came out on his back porch. Barefoot and with hair all tousled, Sam tucked his shirttail into his trousers, speaking as he did so. "The pan was washed yesterday," he said. "There's clean straining cloths in the toolshed and plenty of wood over by the fence. Just make yourself at home. You know as much about molasses making as I do."

"Much obliged," Papa said, getting down from the wagon. Sam went back into the house. The men heard the rattle of a pot against a stove, and soon they smelled coffee perking.

Sam didn't leave his mill with everyone—only a few trusted men—for molasses making was an art. It required a certain touch to produce a syrup with the right color and flavor. Men who lacked that touch made a dark, strong molasses that most folks didn't care for.

The Marshall men made the brightest syrup in the county. The buckets of molasses with which they paid Sam for the use of the mill were always spoken for in advance. There were a few more men who did almost as well. Sam left these men to their own making, and he took a few less buckets from them. The rest of the time Flo Rankin kept the store while Sam made the sorghum.

In the pale darkness of breaking dawn, Rud took Bess from the wagon and put her to the pole that turned the mill. From others years, the gentle mule knew what was expected of her. Rud squatted and fed a handful of cane into the grinder. "Get up," he said. The animal started her patient circling, and the squeaky pole passed over Rud's head each time she made a round. Patiently, man and beast worked together, the livelihood of each dependent on the other. In time the morning star faded into a bright new day, and the tub below the mill spout was full of pale green juice.

Papa went to the toolshed, returning with a white feed sack. The men stretched the cloth across the tub lip, lifted it, and strained the juice into the fifty-gallon vat.

"Get up," Rud said again, taking his place back at the mill. Around and around the mule circled, pausing at intervals, while the men strained juice until the vat was almost full.

Papa built a fire in the furnace under the pan. The smoke seeped out, stinging his eyes. Then the kindling flamed, and the juice began to simmer. When it reached a boil, the sweet-sour steam permeated the valley, and neighbors far up the mountainsides knew someone was making sorghum. By that time the hot sun was peeking over the hills and Sam had opened his store for business. As the day got under way, folks on the way to the store or the gristmill stopped by to see how the molasses was coming along. Women in sunbonnets asked about Lucy, about the operation they had heard Corky might have, and then they went on their way. The men, most of them in overalls, talked about the best sorghum they had ever tasted, about the animal signs they had seen on the way, and sooner or later, each of them wondered when things were going to start picking up. Now and then one of the men took the stirring paddle from Rud, relieving him of the tiring, kneeling position. Eventually they took care of whatever business had brought them to the valley, and the men made their way back up the gutted trails that fingered the hills.

Near noon Rud saw Beard and Af totter into the post office. A few minutes later, they planted themselves on two blocks of wood in the toolhouse shade. Beard, a subscriber to the *Kansas City Star* weekly, unfolded his latest copy and laid it across his lap. He fumbled in his shirt pocket, brought out a pair of gold-rimmed glasses, and tucked the wires around his ears. To read, the old man had to turn his head sideways, to roll the pupils of his eyes from under the whitish crawlers that covered most of his vision. "Farm prices drop sharply. Dry weather blamed for slight increase in food products," he read aloud. A rooster crowed. A wagon rumbled down the road. The juice boiling around the stirring paddle bubbled and popped.

"Bread five cents a loaf. Beefsteak twenty cents a pound." The old man ran a brown tongue over his bushy lips. "I could eat a bellyful of steak," he said.

Rud felt his stomach move; he heard it growl. "You and a million others," he said. A fly, drawn to the sweet smell, lit on Rud's stirring hand. He raised the paddle, and the insect buzzed up and lit on Beard's nose.

"Public works debated in Washington. The devil and

tarnation!" he cried. The old man yanked his glasses from his nose, and the flailing hand knocked the fly into a senseless buzzing around his head. "Washington had better stop debating and do something. If they don't, that feller ain't goin' to get my vote next election. That's for sartin!"

Af, quiet up to that point, gave a weak chuckle. "Chances are you won't be around next election. Know good and well I won't if I don't get to feelin' better. I been bilious the better part of a week now."

Beard put his glasses back in his shirt pocket and dropped the paper on the ground. "It's the weather," he told his friend. "You'll feel better when it cools off."

"It shouldn't be much longer before frost," Af said. "I heard a katydid singing for it on the way over. As I see it, we should be gettin' frost in about two weeks."

"I don't know about that," Beard said. "All my life I been told frost comes six weeks from the time a feller hears katydids. In the long run, it may figure out the same though, 'cause I heard katydids two or three weeks ago. I say the difference in opinion comes from folks not hearin' the insects at the same time. What's your notion on that, Paul?"

Paul Marshall was poking wood into the furnace. He slammed the metal door and, fanning himself with his hat, said, "The best sign I know is the walking-stick insect. I've watched the devil's darning needle for years. Without fail, frost comes six weeks after I see one."

"I don't know much about them darning needles," Af said. "I was always kind of afraid of 'em. But you'll see frost about ten weeks after you hear locusts holler. I can vouch for that."

"There's a bad winter sign I've noticed," Papa said, "one that seems to be in the making right now. Foliage on the trees is mighty dense, and the leaves are getting bright ahead of frost. Notice the reddish color on that cane."

"Early color on plants is a good sign alright," Af agreed.

While Rud stirred and the old men talked, two barefoot boys, one a head taller than the other, sauntered down the store steps. Rud saw them move slowly toward him, their pink tongues licking Black Cow suckers, their faces red, their hair the color of the dead grass about the vat. When they reached Rud's side, the tall one said, "How long you figure this is going to take?"

"From juice to molasses takes about eight hours, depending on the weather. As hot as it is today, it shouldn't take quite that long," Rud said. "Looks like we'll be finished by four."

"My dad will be here next week. I'll be in school by then," the short one said.

"Will Corky be startin' to school?" the tall boy asked.

Rud shook his head. "My wife's going to start teaching him. But we won't have him in shape to start regular school before the first of the year. We're hoping by then—"

"It's shore hot," one of the boys cut in. A little breeze rippled the grass around his dusty feet, but the boy did not feel it, and neither did Rud. He was skimming a greenish scum from the shiny syrup. The steam had increased as the juice thickened, and it was fogging around his face.

Seeking a cool spot, the boys joined the old men in the shade. Children did not stay in Beard's company for long without teasing his imagination. Rud heard one of the boys say, "Is it true you can see the wind if you rub sow's milk in your eyes?"

"Of course it's true," Beard came back, "providin' there's any wind to see."

The short boy bit down on his sucker and then groaned with pain. "I been havin' toothache," he said.

"I'll give you a cure for that," Beard said. "Find you a jawbone of a mule or a horse. Pick the bone up with your teeth and walk backward until the pain stops. I guarantee it'll stop the ache, and the number of steps you have to take before the pain leaves indicates the number of years it will be before the trouble returns."

The boys heard him out; then the short one made some vomiting sounds. The taller one said, "I'd sooner drink sheep manure tea."

"Well," laughed the old man, "if you're going to be like that, I have another remedy. Go to a lightning-struck tree. Get a splinter and pick your tooth until it bleeds. Hide the splinter under the eaves of the house. That'll take care of your problem."

Rud left the paddle with Papa and took his turn at the lunch Lucy had packed for them. Over his drumstick he saw the boys grin in unbelief. But he knew boys well enough to know they would try the latter suggestion.

As the afternoon sun moved across the sky, the liquid dropped lower and lower in the vat. About two o'clock Papa said, "It's time to fan her." He picked up a shovel-like tool and handed it to his son. Rud lifted the syrup and poured it back in the pan.

"Whatcha doin' that for?" the boys wanted to know.

"Fanning brightens the molasses," Rud said.

He continued the lifting and the pouring until Papa said, "They're ready to start slugging." Rud turned the tool sideways and let the syrup drip as a person would test jelly. When the drops trinkled down and became a crystal thread, Pape increased the fire. "It's time for them to quilt," he told the kids.

The boys watched the bubbles become uniform in size and shape. The surface of the boiling molasses looked as if it had been quilted.

When the bubbles began to pop, Rud told Beard to time it for him—to let him know when fifteen minutes had passed. The old man pulled his watch from a pant's pocket on his peg-leg side. When he replaced the timepiece, the molasses was done.

They poured Sam's portion and that which Rud planned to sell into shiny, gallon buckets. They put the rest into a barrel.

Beard and Af helped Papa load the wagon while Rud cleaned up and washed the pan. Then Bess was harnessed to the wagon, and the hot, bone-weary men started back up the mountain toward home.

The sun was easing itself behind the timberline when they got home. Rud stopped the wagon in front of the cellar, and he climbed down from the spring seat.

"There's no reason why we can't unload tomorrow," he said, "Let's take a bath and put on some dry clothes before supper."

Papa agreed, and the men put on their old swimming overalls. Lucy sent a bar of soap and fresh clothes out with Corky. Three giant shadows walked before them when they started to the river.

The Bermuda grass was brittle under their steps, but the cows were nibbling at it on their way to the barn. The lead cow had a bell around her golden neck, and it tinkled as she eased her way along. The calves in the lot could see their mothers, and one, then the other, bawled for them to hurry.

At the incline the earthy smell of the river reached Rud's nose. He took Corky's arm. When they started down the incline, a blue dragonfly kept darting in front of them.

Men and boy waded into the clear stream. Corky practiced swimming, but Rud lathered himself from head to foot and passed the bar to Papa. Rud ducked down to rinse himself off. When he came up, he heard the pitter of falling bark. Several trees away he saw Timid and Shy chasing each other from limb to limb. For several minutes they frolicked in the treetops. Then the female squirrels raced to the forest floor. When Timid caught up with Shy, they rolled over and over, nipping each other like two playful kittens.

Their noisy play attracted a pair of bluejays, and the birds flew down to a swaying limb to referee the scuffle. Finally Timid let go of her smaller sister, and Shy became interested in a caterpillar web, strung between two bushes. She slapped at the web; it snapped loose, covering her with striped caterpillars. Squeaking with surprise, she rolled over and over, adding crushed leaves and sticks to the web. Rud told Corky what had happened.

Knowing how badly Chipper hated having anything on her coat, Corky said, "I wish we could help her."

"She'll be alright," Rud said. "Squirrels have their ways of righting a situation." The words were barely out of his mouth when Timid gave a warning signal that sounded like the firing of a machine gun. "Yak! Yak! Yak!" Instantly, the bluejays took flight. But Little Shy was so disturbed by the mess on her coat that she missed the second needed to dart to safety.

"Yoke! Yoke!" Rud recognized Trumpet's voice. He screamed to the top of his lungs and fell over the smooth round stones in his effort to save the squirrel. But it was too late! The hound had gobbled Shy in one big gulp. Rud had to tell Corky. He tried to soften what had happened by describing animal heaven and God's love for all creatures. But Corky was still crying when they started back across the pasture.

Just before they reached the backyard gate, Lucy came out of the house, milk buckets in hand, and Chipper darted out in front of her. Rud heard her call the pet. In the next instant, he heard the same "Yoke! Yoke!" he had heard a few minutes before.

Lucy screamed. Her milk pails clattered to the ground. Chipper darted under the yard fence. But the hound leaped it, landing a few inches from the squirrel's back. Old Rang heard the commotion and tore around the house, all bristled and barking. But he stopped at the gate and dared his enemy to come back and enter the yard.

Rud ran toward Chipper, and he almost reached her. But the animal so was so crazy with fright, she turned and ran from him. "Yoke! Yoke!" Trumpet was still barking. About every other "Yoke" he nipped the squirrel's tail. In their chase, the Marshalls were strung out like an hysterical caravan—with Rud in the lead, Lucy following Papa, and the sobbing, stumbling Corky bringing up the rear.

At the fence Chipper went under the rail. The hound put his forefeet on top of the fence and tried to throw himself over. All out of breath, Rud caught up with him and managed to get a hold on the dog's tail. He yanked the hound around with all his strength. When Rud let go, Trumpet spun around head over heels. Yelping in pain and disgrace, he scrambled to his feet and headed for home. Rud climbed the fence and called Chipper. Trembling and panting, she circled back to the man. When Rud put the pet in Corky's arms, the joy of having her alive helped him forget the sorrow he had felt over Shy's death.

Chapter Ten

THE SUMMER COMES TO A CLOSE

The lowly grasshopper, like nature's time clock, ticked off the fall days. Rud and Papa picked the cotton—all six hundred pounds of it—and packed it in the back of the truck. "We made less than a half bale," Rud told Lucy, while they were milking. "After ginning, it won't bring more than twenty dollars. But with that added to what I made at the sawmill, what the folks gave us, and the sorghum yet to sell, we'll manage."

While the men were gathering the cotton and the corn, Lucy wrote to Dr. Holt, and the physician made arrangements for Corky's operation. He wrote the Marshalls telling them Corky would have to stay in the hospital for five days. After a healing period at home, he would fit heavy glasses to the boy's eyes. As to how much he would see, only time would tell.

Lucy was too far along to make the rough trip and Rud hated to leave her. But the teacher in Lucy refused to let anything stand in her way of getting Corky ready for school. "Granny will look after me," she said. "We have got to get

Corky ready for school. I've been thinking about what you said—back there in the spring—about finding a suitable name for him. I hate to put Corky on his medical records."

"He must be gettin' close to six," Rud said. "Why don't you give a birthday party—a naming party for us. You know, a cake with a name on top."

"Any suggestions?" Lucy asked.

"Not before we ask Corky. I think the kid will be kind of lucky having something to say in the matter. If things seem right, we'll talk about it tonight."

After supper the family had a conference. Sitting around the table, still ladened with leftovers and dirty dishes, Rud said, "Your mama and me—we have been talkin'. Now that you are gettin' to be a big boy, about ready to start to school, we thought it would be nice if you had another name besides Corky. Like I told your mama, you are lucky to get to choose for yourself. We were wondering if you have a name you like especially well."

Corky put his forefinger in his mouth and fingered a front tooth that had loosened that day. After some thought, he said, "I like Charles."

Rud and Lucy smiled their approval, but they were unprepared for his next statement. "Charles was my name before my other mommie started calling me Corky."

Rud, Papa, and Lucy looked at the child and then stared at one another open-mouthed. Finally, Rud brought his voice down to a casual level, and he said, "Did you have a last name—something besides Charles?"

Again, Corky worked at his tooth. Then his finger came out of his mouth and he grinned up at the man.

"Just Marshall. That's the only last name I got." Rud and Lucy reached for their child, and each gave him a hug. Then they explained the trip he and Rud would take and the hospital stay, following the operation. In keeping with the times, they bypassed the reason Lucy would not be with them. Once again Corky fingered his tooth. Then he said, "Is Mama not going because she's goin' to have a baby?"

Papa gave an embarrassed cough and excused himself. When the front door slammed and he was out of hearing on the front porch, Lucy said, "Who told you about the baby?"

"Bobby Rankin," Corky said. "Bobby said, 'Your mama's going to have a baby.' I said, 'She ain't.'"

"She isn't," Lucy corrected.

"I said, 'I don't believe you,'" Corky continued. "He said, 'She is, but you better not tell.'"

Rud, as tongue-tied as Papa, left the situation in Lucy's hands. "You are getting to be a big boy," she said. "And you guessed right. I can't make the trip with you because it might hurt the baby. But I think it would be better if we kept it our secret."

"Why?" Corky asked. "I think it would be nice to tell the kids. I think it will be nice having a baby."

Again Lucy reached for the child. Holding him close, she said, "I'm glad you want this baby. And it will be nice—very, very nice."

Rud had been so concerned about the medical care for Lucy and the boy, and just plain making a living, that he had not given much thought to the baby as a person. Listening to Lucy and Corky, he visualized for the first time the joy that having a baby could bring.

"We'll take the baby to see the squirrels, won't we, Daddy? And I'll be able to see them too, won't I, Daddy?" Corky said, his voice quivering with excitement.

"That you will—that you will, Charles," Rud said, trying out the new name.

"Charles," Corky repeated. "Charles," he tried the name again. Grinning around a wet forefinger, he said, "Charles tickles my tongue a lot better than Corky." Then he laughed, and Rud decided he was a very handsome child, now that his cheeks were round and his hair had the slightest hint of yellow.

Sunday afternoon, Lucy surprised Corky with a cake and a party that included Esther and the Sunday School class. The children brought him crayons, a pencil, and a tablet.

"Something to pass the time with," Esther said. Then she gave him and Chipper a great big hug.

The next morning Rud piled his suitcase in with the cotton and the buckets of sorghum. Corky kissed Lucy, and he hugged Papa. Rud told them to take care of themselves, and then he headed the truck toward Little Rock.

Rud sold his products at Russellville. When he reached the state capital, he drove to a boardinghouse, where Lucy had arranged for him to stay. He checked Corky into the hospital the next morning, and the boy was operated on the following day.

By the time Corky was fitted with the heavy glasses, October had moved across the landscape, coloring the trees like the basketful of marbles Dr. Holt had given Corky on that final trip. Though the glasses did not give the child normal vision, Corky considered his eyes near perfect, after having been almost blind.

When he had rested from the long trip after returning home, Corky asked Rud to take him to see the squirrels.

A change had taken place since they had last crossed the pasture. Along either side of the path seedpods stood ripe in the crisp but sunny day. Around the rock ledge, runners of orange bittersweet competed with tongues of flaming ivy. The river was full now. The squirrel tree was golden. Overhead, a wedge of geese honked their way southward. Inside the squirrel hole, they could see half a nubbin of corn and some acorns. But the squirrels were nowhere in sight.

"Reckon old Trumpet got them?" Corky asked anxiously.

Rud assured him the dog had not harmed the squirrels. "They're around someplace. I imagine they are busy laying in their winter food."

"Do squirrels hibernate?" Corky asked, using a new word Lucy had taught him.

Rud shook his head. "They will do a lot of sleeping during bad spells. But they will be up and about on warm days. If we don't see them today, we will see them then. Like I told you, they will know where to find nuts in the deepest snow.

Around March there will be little ones again. Sometime between now and then I think we had better help Chipper get used to the wilds. Animals need to be free. They are happier with their own kind."

"I know," Corky said. "Besides, I'll have the baby. I'll have to take care of it." Just then the wind whistled through the trees, and the swaying hickory released a shower of golden leaves. For a second the child stared as though spellbound. Then Rud heard him suck in a deep breath and he cried, "Daddy, Daddy, I see the wind!"

BROADMAN
B P
SUPPLIES

Date Due

Code 4386-04, CLS-4, Broadman Supplies, Nashville, Tenn., Printed in U.S.A.